# The Art of Manifestation
# Astro-Moon Diary
# 2021

from the I Choose Love Series.
The Pathway of the Spiritual Warrior.

# The Art of Manifestation

## Astro-Moon Diary 2021

## This Diary Belongs to

......................................................

The Art of Manifestation Astro-Moon Diary 2021
From the I Choose Love Series
The Pathway of the Spiritual Warrior

The Art of Manifestation Astro-Moon Diary
First Published 2019 A-Z of Emotional Health Ltd.
©2019 Jenny Florence/Burgess The A-Z of Emotional Health Ltd.
Published by the A-Z of Emotional Health Ltd.

The intent of the author is only to offer information of a general nature to assist in an individual's search for emotional and spiritual wellness. In the event that you use any of the information in this book for yourself, the author and publisher assume no responsibility for your actions.

# The Art of Manifestation
## Astro-Moon Diary

## Welcome to 2021

# Contents

My dear friends, what extraordinary times we are living in.
2020 brought a year of circumstances that pushed our global community into a
space of immediate transformation, both individually
and as a collective humanity.

As I write these words, looking ahead to the year of 2021, I wonder, how will we
integrate the lessons so directly brought to us. Can we each as individuals, make
the kinds of choices and decisions that will create a genuinely sustainable future,
not only for us as human beings, but a way of living that honors and respects all
of life that surrounds us and of which we are an integral part.

My deepest respect goes out to you all, for in using books and resources like this,
you make a personal choice to walk a conscious path in alignment with the
natural energy of the greater universal consciousness, the stuff of the stars and
the very substance of who we are.


Namaste

# The Art of Manifestation

The art of manifestation involves not only imagining and dreaming of the kind of life that we wish to have, we must also take actions that enable our dreams to find form. Our state of mind, our attitudes and perceptions, and the way that we feel, our emotions, all have an impact on our ability to fully immerse ourselves in this creative process.

It seems to me that manifestation has its own cyclical and natural pattern of evolution.

- We listen to our desires, and we allow ourselves to dream.
- We imagine possibilities and we honor their potential.
- We evaluate and decide what steps we must take to initiate these possibilities into form.
- Remaining open to ongoing evaluation, we commit to a pathway forward.
- We persevere in our doing, trusting that any diversions and interruptions are sent to us to bring greater meaning, clarity, and direction.
- When needed, whether in our external actions or deep within our own psyche, we identify any ongoing work that we need to do to keep the energy flowing.
- We continue our ongoing pathway of evolution and co-creativity, and we trust that we will always be shown the next steps.
- Listening to the wisdom and guidance of the universe, when needed we course correct.
- Trusting that the universe knows of our fullest potential and holds a higher vision for us that is greater than we ourselves could possibly imagine, we understand that we will be given what we need, although not always necessarily what we want.
- Our pathway emerges and our dreams begin to take form.

# How to Use this Diary

**The Art of Manifestation and the Influence of the Moon.**

Given that the magnetic pull of the Moon is sufficiently powerful to move our oceans, and that we as human beings are made up of around 70% water, it makes perfect sense to recognize that this powerful magnetic force will have an impact on us all. For anyone who is interested in enhancing their skills of conscious manifestation, it makes sense to take some time to understand how this influence affects us each as individuals and to capitalize on these cycles of incoming energy.

In the ocean of our lives, it can be incredibly helpful to know, when to surf the waves, when to tread water or learn to float, when to swim against the tide, or indeed, if we find ourselves in deep water, when to become a diver.

One of the best ways of learning to align and work with the incoming energy of the Moon and her connection with the incoming energy from any of the other planets, is to learn to listen to ourselves and to notice how we find ourselves thinking, feeling and responding to these incoming influences.

To do this, we will need to be aware of where the Moon is during her monthly cycle, along with some awareness of her relationships with the other planets as well.

This diary is designed to help you to do exactly this.

Each month as well as highlighting key phases of the Moon, you will also find further information about the incoming energy and potential influences of some of the other major collaborations and planetary connections. Plus additional guidance from Oracle Cards and Runes for every month.

Alongside the daily calendar dates which can be used as a standard diary, you will also find additional pages for you to journal and record your own experiences.

The more that you do this, the more you will be able to recognize the way in which these influences affect you in a personal way, allowing you to understand and work with the incoming energy on an ongoing basis, finetuning your ability to become consciously co-creative on your personal journey of manifestation.

At the beginning of this book you will find information about the different phases of the moon and the way that you can use and understand these natural cycles as part of the process of manifestation, including the impact of both solar and lunar eclipses, plus a description of the way that the lunar energy is affected and channeled as the moon travels through each sign of the zodiac. I have also explained the potential impact of the influences of Mercury, Venus and Mars in retrograde, and listed the dates that these events occur.

There is also a section on the turning of the seasons, the Solstices and Equinoxes. For thousands of years the wisdom traditions have marked and celebrated the changing of the seasons, honoring and appreciating the shifts in energy that take place during these times and so I have also shared some thoughts about the solstices and the equinoxes and the way in which we can utilize the energy of these pivotal moments of natural transition to support us in becoming consciously co-creative.

By recording your own experiences, as you journey through the year, this diary will form a personal record for you to continue to build upon and deepen your understanding of how to align yourself with the natural rhythms of the this extraordinary planet and her relationship with the energy of the planets that surround us.

For anyone who is serious about manifesting in alignment with the natural planetary influences you may also wish to use the Art of Manifestation Astro-Moon Journal.

The diary and journal can be used independently of one another but also compliment and work alongside each other. Both contain information about the Phases of the Moon, the Influence of the Zodiac, Lunar and Solar Eclipses and the Retrograde Planets, however the journal has a more in depth monthly run down of the incoming astro-energies, with additional information about the New and Full Moon influences. There is also a specific emphasis on placing New Moon wishes.

# The Phases of the Moon

**The New Moon.**

The new moon is traditionally associated with the setting of intentions and so the energy at this time naturally invites us to meditate into a space of possibility. If you are a daily meditator, you may already find that for the two days before and the two days after the new moon, your mind may be inclined to wander during your meditations.

If this is the case you may find it helpful to have a pen and paper close by, or use the journaling pages in this diary to make a note of any ideas that come to you during your meditation practice. Personally, during this phase of the moon, I find myself naturally drawn to walking meditations.

Consciously make the effort to spend time outdoors and immerse yourself in nature and whatever your preferred way of finding stillness, calm your mind, and enter your own dreamtime. Let your mind wander into the depths of the new moon energy and give yourself permission to dream big!

**The Crescent Moon.**

In the phase of the crescent moon the seeds that emerged at the new moon will begin to whisper to you, calling to be heard. How we respond to this inner calling will have a direct influence on our ability to be proactive in our developing process of manifestation.

Take your yearnings and your desires seriously and notice any thinking patterns that may be holding you back or limiting your perspectives. In the process of manifestation, we are both doers and deciders and so the extent of our external manifestations will always be a reflection of our ability to embrace our inner growth. At this time, any resistance to change can be identified, paving the way for this month's cycle of inner growth.

The crescent moon invites us to identify any resistances within us, any patterns of thinking or self-sabotaging attitudes and behaviors that may limit us from stepping into the fullest potential of our dreams. Our very recognition of these patterns will automatically diminish their power as well as opening up opportunities and avenues of potential healing and resolution.

## The First Quarter Moon.

The first quarter moon is sometimes thought of as a time when hurdles and obstacles that need to be overcome, will push forwards and enter into our awareness. Personally, I have found that the energy of the first quarter moon affects me in a far more vibrant and positive way.

During this phase of the moon, having identified any inner blocks to progress, during the crescent moon, the seeds of ideas that were planted at the new moon, push themselves forwards in abundance, and I find myself flooded with thoughts of what I will need to do to nurture the possibilities of the new moon, to enable them to begin to take shape and manifest into real form.

I look carefully at the scope of my ideas and begin to focus on those which are most important for me to initiate at this moment in time. The combination of the seeds of the new moon and the learning discovered at the crescent moon, enables me to prioritize and to formulate my actions for the coming month.

## The Gibbous Moon.

In the time of the gibbous moon energy is building, passions are high, and dreams are calling to be made real. Ideas begin to take shape, and the pathway forward gains clarity. Taking time to hold my intentions and my vision for the future in mind, I ground myself in the present moment, and I request guidance in knowing which steps to take in the here and now, before turning my decisions into acts of doing.

Take time to celebrate the joy to be found in the excitement of anticipation, whilst remaining present and grounded. Hold your vision but treasure the here and now moments of your journey and be available to receive guidance. Stay on track, but simultaneously be open to any course corrections that you are guided towards.

## The Full Moon.

The power and energy of the full moon is extraordinary. For anyone who works with healing stones and crystals, be sure to place them outside overnight to recharge in the eliminating power of the full moon. Their energy of release and repair will be revitalized for any healing work over the coming month.

The full brightness of this powerful and highly charged energy brings a space of authenticity where all is revealed and illuminated, and so the full moon is often a time when we experience heightened and intense emotions.

Be kind to yourself and others. Notice and listen, particularly to any situations that are not okay. Things that are usually tolerated or brushed under the carpet will surface and request your attention. So, if you find yourself experiencing any challenging emotions please take them seriously.

The energy of this phase of the moon brings a wonderful opportunity to notice, to listen, to reflect, and then to release and let go, clearing the way to move forwards.

In the process of manifestation, if we find ourselves unable to move forwards or feel stuck in some way, it is often some aspect of our past that is still lingering, blocking us from believing in ourselves or believing in others or finding trust in the possibility of a different future. Anyone who has ever experienced trauma or abuse will tell you that whilst the physical scars will heal, it is the emotional ones that remain.

The full moon illuminates our emotions highlighting exactly what is working for us... as well as anything that is not!

Learn to differentiate between emotions that connect to past experiences, as opposed to emotions that are part of your immediate response system helping you to navigate your life in the here and now. There is a difference!

Our emotions contain and generate energy. Understanding this difference between past and present emotional influences allows you to identify anything that you need to release from the past, empowering you to channel any highly charged emotional energy into positive action.

If you find yourself struggling with challenging emotional states, you may find 'Mindfulness Meets Emotional Awareness - 7 steps to learn the language of your emotions' a useful read. This book explains exactly how and why our most challenging emotions serve us and will teach you how to transform and channel any highly charged emotions into actions that support your pathway rather than hinder it.

## The Disseminating Moon.

As the energy of the full moon diminishes, emotions are released, and forgiveness is discovered. This phase of the moon brings opportunity to step into a position of authentic empowerment. Within this energetic space of emergence, we hold awareness of ourselves, of others and in alignment with the collective soul of humanity, the disseminating Moon invites us to be all that we can be.

This is a time to acknowledge and validate the extraordinariness of who you are, and of everything, both good and bad, that has led you to the place that you stand today and contributed to the person that you are.

Be steady in your actions and in your doings. Stand in your power and be your true self with joy, gratitude, and humility. Let the energy of the disseminating moon filter into every cell of your body, affirming your dedication to your pathway.

## The Last Quarter Moon.

The energy of the last quarter moon invites us to walk our talk. If the full moon energy gives us an opportunity to upgrade our system, letting go of anything that no longer serves us, then the last quarter moon is a time that invites us to integrate our learning and to follow it through in all that we do and in all that we are.

The energy of this moon brings us the opportunity to make sure that our plans, actions and decisions are congruent with all that we wish to be and all that we wish to see in the world.

Stand firm and pay attention to the details of your world and notice if any adjustments need to be made. From a spiritual perspective, do you need to cross any T's or dot any I's to ensure that in all areas of your life, you are living in congruence with your truest values and deepest desires. Within the unique circumstances of your own process of co-creativity are you 'being' everything that you wish to attract for yourself.

For example, how positive are your thoughts? Does your inner critic offer constructive feedback or harsh criticism? Are you kinder to others than to yourself? ... or is it the other way around?

Centre yourself in compassion, kindness, and above all... in love.

## The Balsamic Moon.

The balsamic Moon asks you to trust. Hold your vision, and yet simultaneously let go of any attachment to specific outcomes. This is a time of preparation and nurture, a time to fertilize the ground in anticipation of the coming new moon and of any new seeds that you may wish to sow.

Keep your energy clean and be particularly aware of your personal energetic resonance. Self-responsibility can be understood to mean 'our ability to be responsive to ourselves'. From an energetic perspective, be sure to cleanse yourself of anything that clings and that may no longer be serving you. Centre yourself in the knowledge that as this monthly lunar phase comes to its completion, you can engage in preparing the ground for your own deliverance, making space within for the emergence of a new cycle of opportunity.

Validate, acknowledge, and cherish all that you have achieved during this last phase of manifestation, and in your reflections, remember that there is no wrong way. Anything that appears to have been a wrong turn or a mistake will have led you to exactly the place that you need to be, right now, bringing you the awareness that you needed to take fresh new steps as we approach the coming energy of the next new moon.

# The Moon in the Zodiac Signs

**Moon in Aries.**

At this emotionally powerful time, use the energy to be assertive and to initiate your ideas. Say how it is and take action.

**Moon in Taurus.**

Grounded, sensual and earthy, use this energy to attune yourself with the natural rhythms of nature. A great time for walking meditations.

**Moon in Gemini.**

A time of communication, reaching out and connecting with others, use this energy for networking and socializing.

**Moon in Cancer.**

A wonderful time to be at home, share food and be in the company of family and close friends. Use this energy to nourish your soul, spending time with those you love.

**Moon in Leo.**

Sing, laugh, express yourself and find your voice. Use this energy to feel alive and embrace the joy of self-discovery and self-expression. We are never too old to play!

**Moon in Virgo.**

This energy supports us in attending to any work that requires dedication, structure, order and precision. Approach your tasks with willingness and a desire to serve.

**Moon in Libra.**

The energy of this moon calls us to seek harmony and to find balance. This is a time to share and to discover ourselves through our relationships and the company of others.

**Moon in Scorpio.**

A time to journey inwards, this energy connects us to the depths of our unconscious and can bring deep emotions to the surface. Be sure to listen to yourself and take your yearnings seriously.

**Moon in Sagittarius.**

The energy of this moon invites us to vision in an optimistic future, full of hope and possibility. A great time to expand our horizons and dream big!

**Moon in Capricorn.**

The energy of this moon invites us to take pragmatic, practical actions to manifest our ideas into form. Get building and embrace the joy of doing.

**Moon in Aquarius.**

A time to collaborate, share ideas and work together. The energy of this moon invites you to align your individual contribution with a higher vision of greater purpose that will also serve the collective Soul of humanity.

**Moon in Pisces.**

A time to dream and a time to heal. Open yourself to divine inspiration and allow yourself to be guided. The energy of this moon brings illumination, fuelling imagination and creativity.

# Solar and Lunar Eclipses

During eclipse season, the already intense energy of both the new and full moons are intensified. An eclipse in your sign, will always be a significant trigger point or turning point in your own personal process of evolution and can often herald random events that create sudden and unexpected changes.

On your personal journey of manifestation, understanding this heightened and intensified energy can be incredibly helpful in knowing, when to reflect and set your intentions, and when to take action to move something forwards, particularly if you intend to make or initiate significant changes in any aspect of your life.

Eclipses are also associated with our Karmic journey, creating an energetic rift that overrides our usual perception and connection to time. The energy of the eclipses is said to open an energetic portal that assists us in connecting with our purpose and calling in this present lifetime.

Symbolized in the tarot pack by the cards of Death and the Tower, the energy of both the solar and lunar eclipses are associated with transformation, either internally or in the circumstances of our external lives, and often involves both endings and new beginnings.

When we learn to work with the influence of the eclipses, rather than trying to control events, we consciously make time to allow the energy of a greater universal consciousness to flow through us, bringing us the guidance that we need to support the evolution of our Soul within our human experience.

**Solar Eclipse.**

A solar eclipse is when the moon sits in between the sun and the earth, with the moon covering the sun. This will always occur at a new moon. The energy associated with this time is the same as a new moon, but intensified, like a new moon on steroids!

This is the perfect time to get still and to meditate into a space of personal dreamtime and allow your ideas to flow.

The energy of the solar eclipse can bring an extraordinary surge of creative possibilities, although these may not always arrive in the shape or form that we expect. If you are already involved in setting intentions, but then find that something happens to suddenly create a shift in your direction, trust that this unexpected change is important to your personal growth and evolution, and connected to the calling of your soul.

In matters of manifestation, the universe will always have the upper hand and tends to bring us what we need... although not always what we want!

When we can allow ourselves to trust that even in moments of upheaval and disruption we are being gifted with an opportunity, we open ourselves to receive the fullest potential and the greatest learning to be found in every situation.

**Lunar Eclipse.**

A lunar eclipse is when the earth sits between the moon and the sun, and this will always occur at a full moon. Full moons are associated with heightened emotions and during a lunar eclipse, emotions can run high, like a full moon on steroids!

If we think of the moon as our Feminine Guardian who circles our planet, gathering the energy of the sun and redistributing it to the earth in various measures, at the time of a Lunar Eclipse, the energy of the moon is like a fully charged battery, highly charged and ready to ignite change.

In the full illumination of the moon at her most powerful, all is revealed. Anything and everything that is running smoothly and working in service of a balanced and authentic life will be apparent to us, confirming that we are walking the right path. Likewise, anything and everything that is not working for us or no longer serves us, both internally and externally, will also be brought into the light, calling to be addressed, changed, and if necessary, released.

As long as something remains hidden or unconscious, we are helpless to address the issue and to take actions of resolution, however, when we identify a problem, the very fact that we can see the issue clearly creates an opportunity to seek solutions and find ways forward. On our personal journey of manifestation, the energy of a lunar eclipse increases our connections with any emotional residue from the past that may be clinging and coloring our perspectives inappropriately, creating an amazing opportunity for cleansing and release, clearing the way for resolution and healing. This is a powerful time to embrace forgiveness, of both ourselves and others.

Lunar eclipses are often associated with external changes that are a mirror or a reflection of our internal growth and learning. Whatever is taking place around you, if something in your life appears to be needing to change or to leave, let go gracefully and know that it is timely to the evolution of your soul.

If you are naturally a highly empathic person and particularly sensitive to the feelings of others, at the time of a lunar eclipse you may find yourself highly absorbent to the emotional states of the people around you. Be sure to cleanse and do a daily release ceremony to let go of anything that doesn't belong to you before meditating into your own space of illumination.

- 26 May – 11.19 GMT - Full Moon Lunar Eclipse 5°29' Sagittarius
- 10 June – 10.43 GMT - New Moon Solar Eclipse 19°42' Gemini
- 19 November – 09.04 GMT - Full Moon Lunar Eclipse 27°17' Taurus
- 04 December – 07.34 GMT New Moon Solar Eclipse 12°16' Sagittarius

# The Planets in Retrograde 2021

## The Inner Planets, Mercury and Venus.

**Mercury in Retrograde.**

- 30<sup>th</sup> January 26° Aquarius – 21<sup>st</sup> February 11° Aquarius
- 29<sup>th</sup> May 24° Gemini – 22<sup>nd</sup> June 16° Gemini
- 27<sup>th</sup> September 25° Libra – 18<sup>th</sup> October 10° Libra

The energy of Mercury in retrograde is often associated with obstructions and delays, and in our target and goal orientated culture, we understandably tend to experience this period through a negative lens. Mercury retrograde periods seem to cause us no end of disruption, our plans go astray, we experience roadblocks and diversions, and there are often difficulties with our IT and communication systems.

However, if we step away from this viewpoint and consider that all aspects of planetary influences can support us and bring us valuable and necessary gifts, this shift in our perspective enables us to stand back and work with the incoming energy.

If there is a diversion, then the universe may be giving you a sign, perhaps you are meant to take an alternative route where you will discover something that was absolutely essential to your personal growth and evolution.

If something from your past raises its head during a Mercury retrograde period, then your attention is required. This is an invitation for you to acknowledge this issue and take time to embark on the necessary steps to lay it to rest.

There will always be times in our lives when the energy is with us to set targets and remain fixed on our course, to plough forwards and to push and to strive, however, given that the energy of Mercury represents our capacity to develop and integrate wisdom on our souls' journey within the human experience, when the Winged Messenger of the Gods temporarily stands still in the heavens and appears to travel backwards, this energy calls us back and asks us to slow down, to take our time and to be alert to any signals and signs that the universe is trying to show us.

**Venus in Retrograde.**

- 19th December 26° Capricorn – 29th January 2022 11° Capricorn

Are you in balance? Do you allow yourself to receive as much as you give and vice versa? Are you actively involved in your own self-care? Do you pause to celebrate your achievements along the way, and do you give yourself an appropriate amount of time out to relax?

Self-care is not an act of selfishness; it is an act of consciousness.

When Venus moves into retrograde the energy of the feminine invites you to listen to your heart, to override the demands of a busy mind and be centered in your truest values, including and especially your own self-care.

Venus is in retrograde is a wonderful time to reflect and to realign and rebalance all areas of your life. This revitalizing influence of this phase will keep your energy clean and flowing and ensure that your energetic resonance is congruent with all that you wish to manifest into the world. As such, Venus in retrograde plays an essential role in our ability to manifest our truest desires.

During periods of transition, if you have ever found yourself questioning what your true calling might be, when Venus is in retrograde, ask for guidance and be open to receive.

If during this time you find yourself called to stand up for your values, the female warrior energy of Venus will support you in connecting with the lioness within. In the name of kindness, compassion and peace, her retrograde energy will encourage you to find your authentic voice, speak the truth, and stand firm in your boundaries.

## The Transpersonal Planets, Jupiter and Saturn.

**Jupiter in Retrograde.**

- 20th June 02° Pisces – 18th October 22° Aquarius

A time of powerful personal growth, Jupiter in retrograde invites us on an inward quest of self-discovery seeking the knowledge and illumination that will enable us to stand in our own truth and walk our talk.

Jupiter is known as the planet of good luck and good fortune and from the perspective of manifestation, during the retrograde period we can expect to have experiences that cause us to look within and seek answers of a Spiritual nature.

The Jupiter retrograde energy helps us to forge our true values and to attune with our greater purpose and as such, during this period, windows of opportunity may open that illuminate issues from the past, including past lives, presenting us with the opportunity to find resolution and align with our true calling at this present moment of our journey.

Any internal growth and changes made during this time will then in turn, manifest outwardly and Jupiter returns to a forward flow of expansion.

**Saturn in Retrograde.**

- **23rd May 13° Aquarius – 11th October 06° Aquarius**

When the planet Saturn, known as Father Time and the planet of Karma, moves into retrograde, any aspects of our lives that need restructuring and reorganizing will come to a head.

We will be shown exactly what is working in our lives, alongside any aspects of our world that are not!

The lessons of Saturn can feel quite harsh as the energy calls us to account, speaking in the name of "Tough Love", however, the Saturn retrograde energy is not without reward!

The more open we are to embracing the natural evolutionary process of "weeding and pruning", letting go gracefully of anything that no longer serves us or has outlived its purpose, whether these are physical aspects of our lives or indeed any internal attitudes and beliefs,  then the more smoothly these periods of profound transition will emerge.

The words "emergence" and "emergency" both come from the same source.

Saturn retrograde energy reminds us that change is both necessary and natural and that we live in a continual space of learning, not only from those wonderful experiences that fill us with joy, but also from the experiences that do not feel good and do not resonate with us.

From the perspective of manifestation a valuable part of our ability to become consciously and actively co-creative in our lives is to be able to recognize and listen to all of our experiences, both good and bad, and to use the more challenging ones as a source of inspiration and guidance.

Rather than dwell on the negative, we can use the information from that experience to define our desires with greater clarity. This in turn opens us to receive the guidance and direction that we need to manifest those desires that resonate with us at a core level of Soul.

## The Outer Planets, Uranus, Neptune and Pluto.

The energy of the outer planets is slow moving which means that their influence is deep and penetrating creating significant growth stages with long term implications. In our individual natal charts, the positioning of these planets will not only have personal implications but will also be an indicator of generational traits.

### Uranus in Retrograde.

- 15th August 2020 10° Taurus – 14th January 06° Taurus
- 20th August 14° Taurus – 18th January 2022 10° Taurus

Uranus is known as the Great Awakener and the bringer of sudden changes. I always see his energy as a Lightening Spirit bringing us those thunderbolt moments where we know in no uncertain terms that something needs to change. The energy might arrive as a light bulb moment that opens a window of opportunity for change, however it can also arrive in unexpected and disruptive circumstances, shaking us out of our complacency and pushing us to take actions that free us from

When in retrograde, the impulsive and volatile energy that brings us those important and necessary wake up calls, slows down and invites us to take conscious innovative actions to forge new ways of being and living that can liberate us from limiting perspectives. This energy when harnessed is particularly relevant to establishing liberation and equality for the greater collective.

### Neptune in Retrograde.

- 25th June 23° Pisces – 1st December 20° Pisces

Neptune is the planet of creativity, dreams and imagination and as such plays a key role in manifestation. Being so dreamy, the influence of Neptunian energy opens us to divine guidance and Spiritual illumination supporting us on our pathway of the discovery of our true calling.

However, the duality of Neptune can also create an energetic in which we struggle to hold our boundaries, lose touch with reality, or become absorbed in illusion, creating a vulnerability to those who operate through delusion and deception.

When in retrograde, the Neptunian energy calls us to get real!

Bringing a level of illumination that offers a kind of Spiritual Reality check, we can see beyond the illusions that may have previously been holding us back, and use these powerful insights to initiate new pathways of creativity level to support and fuel our process of manifestation.

**Pluto in Retrograde.**

- **27th April 26° Capricorn – 6th October 24° Capricorn**

The energy of Pluto transforms through the natural cycle of death and re-birth and offers a powerful energetic of change. His intense volcanic energy takes us deep into the unconscious, showing us any shadows from the past that need to be released.

Pluto naturally invites us to harness the energy of personal reflection at its most powerful, bringing us an understanding of our psychological make-up so we may face our deepest issues, purify and release, emerging afresh with greater vitality and potency.

In our process of manifestation, Pluto retrograde energy invites us to surrender to that which we are shown and to reflect on those deep inner issues that rise from the unconscious desiring change and evolution.

This is not a time to hold onto or cling to the past. If some aspect of your world seems to be coming to an end, whether internal or external, such as any outdated thinking patterns or behaviors, an inappropriate or limiting belief, or an actual situation or person, let go gracefully and allow yourself to emerge into a space of new beginnings.

## Chiron and the Consciousness of Healing.

### Chiron in Retrograde.

- 27<sup>th</sup> April 26° Capricorn – 6<sup>th</sup> October 24° Capricorn

Chiron embodies the classic architype of the wounded healer. In mythology he is depicted as half man and half beast, able to bring wisdom and to teach and heal others and yet he cannot heal himself.

Astrologically, Chiron is not a planet, but a comet, whose presence here is transient. Energetically it is said that his presence will create a rainbow bridge that will lead humanity to a higher plane of consciousness inviting us to stand in equality, not only alongside one another, but in unity with all of life. As an outer influence, his energy is slow moving and therefore can signify profound generational changes.

It is also interesting that many Tribal cultures hold legends that speak of all of the life on this planet arriving on the tail of a comet, validating the perspective that we all come from the same source and are all equal.

The retrograde energy of Chiron invites us to engage in a process of deep cleansing and release, laying the past to rest and stepping into a space of unity and higher vision. This is the kind of healing that carries the potential for us both as individuals and as a collective humanity to resolve long standing historical wounds that have spanned generations, bringing us deep and lasting healing in mind body and soul.

# The Solstices and Equinoxes

At these pivotal moments in the natural cycles of time, it is as though the energy of the Earth pauses for breath. It is as though the space between heaven and earth becomes fluid, translucent and free of clutter. These shifts in time and space offer an extraordinary opportunity to achieve and access higher levels of consciousness and awareness.

During the four days either side of these powerful shifts we can often receive profound downloads of illumination, leading to an increase in our intuitive abilities, heightening our ability to channel and connect with source energy, divine inspiration and with the greater consciousness.

These pivotal moments in time bring extraordinary opportunities to reach a higher vision or viewpoint that can change our perceptions and perspectives, freeing us from limiting beliefs and bringing clarity of mind and new direction.

These periods are the perfect opportunity to engage in any spiritual practice that supports your personal growth and awareness and offer the ideal time to create ceremonies of appreciation, gratitude and celebration, as part of your manifestation process.

As well as the Solstices and the Equinoxes, during the year there are four other pivotal turning points which were understood and celebrated in the Celtic and Pagan traditions.

Exactly the same energetic principles apply and depending on whether you are in the northern or southern hemisphere, your ceremonies and celebrations at this time will vary, tuning you to the rhythm of the seasons of your own geographical area.

During these pivotal moments of natural transition, use this diary to check in with the incoming astrological energy, and allow yourself the time to meditate and take full advantage of the intensified energetic possibilities to enhance your personal process of manifestation.

-------------------------------------------------- Journaling & Notes --------------------------------------------------

29

-------------------------------------------- Journaling & Notes --------------------------------------------

# Welcome to January 2021

Astrologically, January looks to be an intense and dynamic month and is literally an invitation to be the change that we wish to see in the world!

During January the expansive and encouraging energy of Jupiter and the firm and structured energy of Saturn, who has been calling us to re-structure over the past 18 months, both now journeying through Aquarius, will square up to the energy of Uranus, the great awakener and bringer of sudden changes.

The energy of **the New Moon on the 13th in Capricorn** holds this intense encounter with added fire from the warrior planet of Mars, aligning beautifully with **this month's Oracle Cards of Leadership, and Choices and Decisions.** This stunning duo give a very clear indication of how best to harness the astro-energy this month, particularly when setting our New Moon wishes, dreams and intentions.

**Our Runes this month, of Hagalaz, the Rune of Disruption and Kano, the Rune of Openings** combine with the messages in these cards, inviting us to align our thoughts, words and actions  with all that we wish to see and manifest in the world, acknowledging that our free will and conscious choice holds the key to our personal empowerment within a changing world.
We hold this vision as **the Sun enters Aquarius on the 19th.**

As we move through January the energy intensifies, culminating with **the Full Moon in Leo on the 28th,** when Uranus the great awakener aligns with Mars, the masculine Warrior Planet and also Lilith, whose energy shows us our vulnerabilities and connects us to those deep desires that we often struggle to openly acknowledge. We also simultaneously enter the Mercury Retrograde shadow. (for detailed information on Mercury in Retrograde see page 24)

This collaboration suggests situations that will highlight and bring to our awareness any personal issues that we need to address to bring our own pathway into alignment with the greater collective vision of the future, and also any global changes that need to be made, with an invitation for us each to use ourselves as a source of empowerment and to act for the good of the whole, rather than simply focusing on our individual needs.

he Rune of Hagalaz speaks of disruption aligned with a greater purpose, suggesting circumstances that create an awakening, either personally or globally or both. The greater the disruption, the more necessary it is for your personal growth and evolution.

Leadership

30

We all lead by example,
our words and actions presenting a role model to
everyone that we come into contact with.
This card asks you to take an ownership of
your personal leadership qualities and to align your
thoughts, words and actions with everything
that you wish to see in the world.

**Additional messages and guidance.**
This card invites you to be the change you wish to see in the world.
Align yourself with your true core values and step into the greatest version of you in every aspect of your world. By demonstrating your core values in everything that you do, in your thoughts, in your words, and in your actions, you provide a role model to others.

If this card is drawn in response to a specific question which involves you stepping into a position of greater leadership, this card is here to validate your leadership qualities and encourage you to move forwards with confidence.

The Rune of Kano speaks of renewed clarity, clear intentions and an opening that enables mutual growth in relationships through awareness and understanding. It often suggests that we will be shown some aspect of our lives that was previously hidden from view that needs to change.

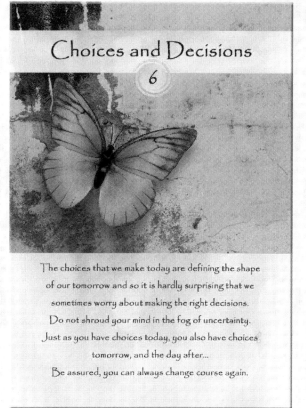

Choices and Decisions

6

The choices that we make today are defining the shape of our tomorrow and so it is hardly surprising that we sometimes worry about making the right decisions. Do not shroud your mind in the fog of uncertainty. Just as you have choices today, you also have choices tomorrow, and the day after... Be assured, you can always change course again.

**Additional messages and guidance.**
Do you overburden yourself in the process of making decisions, creating an internal stream of thoughts that try to anticipate every potential outcome for fear of making the wrong choice?

In truth, there is no such thing as a wrong choice or a wrong decision. None of us can actually know how something will be until we get there and try it on for size! This is how we learn and grow and discover the things that work for us, as well as the things that do not, helping us to find clarity in our future decisions and choices. An essential part of the process of manifestation.

**28** Monday
Gemini

**29** Tuesday
Gemini / Cancer

Full Moon LA 19.28 – NY 22.28

**30** Wednesday
Cancer

Full Moon London 03.28 – Sydney 14.28 – Auckland 16.28

**31** Thursday
Cancer / Leo

New Year's Eve

**1** Friday
Leo

New Year's Day

——————————————— Journaling and Notes ———————————

---------------------------------------------------------------------------------------------------------

**2** Saturday
Leo

---------------------------------------------------------------------------------------------------------

**3** Sunday
Leo / Virgo

**4** Monday
Virgo

**5** Tuesday
Virgo / Libra

Full Moon LA 19.28 – NY 22.28

**6** Wednesday
Libra

Last Quarter Moon

**7** Thursday
Libra / Scorpio

**8** Friday
Scorpio

—————————— Journaling and Notes ——————————

-------------------------------------------------------------------------------

**9** Saturday
**Scorpio / Sagittarius**

-------------------------------------------------------------------------------

**10** Sunday
**Sagittarius**

**11** Monday
**Sagittarius / Capricorn**

**12** Tuesday
**Capricorn**

**New Moon LA 21.00**

**13** Wednesday
**Capricorn / Aquarius**

**New Moon NY 00.00 London 05.00 – Sydney 16.00 – Auckland 18.00**

**14** Thursday
**Aquarius**

**15** Friday
**Aquarius / Pisces**

Journaling and Notes

---

**16** Saturday
Pisces

---

**17** Sunday
Pisces

## 18 Monday
**Pisces / Aries**

**Martin Luther King Day**

## 19 Tuesday
**Aries**

**Sun enters Aquarius**

## 20 Wednesday
**Aries / Taurus**

**First Quarter Moon**

## 21 Thursday
**Taurus**

## 22 Friday
**Taurus**

Journaling and Notes

**23** Saturday
**Taurus / Gemini**

**24** Sunday
**Gemini**

**25** Monday
Gemini / Cancer

**26** Tuesday
Cancer

**27** Wednesday
Cancer

**28** Thursday
Cancer / Leo

Full Moon LA 11.16 – NY 14.16 – London 19.16

**29** Friday
Leo

Full Moon Sydney 06.16 - Auckland 08.16

———————————— Journaling and Notes ————————————

----------------------------------------------------------------------------------------------------

**30** Saturday
Leo / Virgo

**Mercury in Retrograde until 21st February**
----------------------------------------------------------------------------------------------------

**31** Sunday
Virgo

---------------------------------------------------- Journaling & Notes ----------------------------------------------------

# Welcome to February 2021

The overall energy of February calls us to develop tolerance and to truly value and appreciate our differences as a space of learning. And as always, our Oracle Cards and Runes align beautifully with this energetic. **Our Runes of Gebo, the Rune of Partnership and Berkana, the Rune of Growth, join our Oracle Cards of Mistakes, and Be your Brilliant Self**, calling us to consider and value all aspects of partnership and relationship as a space of growth and learning, including our relationship with ourselves.

The pressures of the planetary influences from January continue to build, with alignments taking place at the time of **the New Moon in Aquarius on the 11ᵗʰ** that invite us to review any aspects of our lives that are out of balance. Whether in the immediacy of our unique individual lives, in our communities, or as a global collective humanity, much is being shown to us at this time, with a calling to embrace changes that align with a higher vision. In the buildup to the New Moon, dive into your dreamtime and allow your mind to wander. Imagine the shape of the world that you wish to create and allow yourself to dream of a future vision. Where do you wish to be in ten years time… in five years time… in a year… how might your life look in the future?

**Manifestation involves noticing, thinking, dreaming, allowing and doing. The first few weeks of February are an excellent time to stand back from our western goal driven orientation and practice the art of allowing, responding to what we are shown. Remain humble and ground yourself in the extraordinariness of everyday living. The doing will come later in the month.**

With **Mercury in Retrograde**, delays and diversions may well appear to halt your progress, however when we understand these periods as an invitation for reflection, then even during periods of energetic intensity, we can make use of these times to invest in our meditative practice, incorporating mindfulness into our everyday lives in real terms. We can expect a significant energy shift around **the 21ˢᵗ when Mercury Stations Direct** sitting midway between Saturn and Jupiter. This marks an energetic turning point and in the week leading up to **the Full Moon in Virgo on the 27ᵗʰ** the energy is particularly productive and supports us in taking actions that initiate and create the kind of environment in which our dreams can begin to germinate with the potential to manifest in the longer term future. The last week of February is a time to do!

The Rune of Gebo, or Partnership, is also sometimes referred to as A Gift. It reminds us that healthy partnerships and relationships recognize the unique individuality of all parties, with an awareness that respectful appreciation of our differences is both inspirational and a gift.

## MISTAKES
### (34)

If you feel you have made a mistake
or indeed someone else has done so with impact on you,
please do not feel bad about this.
Treasure and value your mistakes and those of others
around you. They are the cutting edge of our personal
growth and evolution. Lean into the learning and
celebrate your openness to grow.

**Additional messages and guidance.**
Are you experiencing an overload of challenging emotions, criticism and judgement on the basis of either your own mistakes or those of someone else? Remaining tangled in the negative emotional aftermath of any situation will hold you back and cloud your vision, coloring your perspectives and influencing your ability to move forwards. Let go of any form of judgement and honor your right and entitlement to make mistakes and offer the same to others.
You are a wonderful human being, and your mistakes are vital steppingstones in the process of your growth and evolution, enhancing your ability
to grow into the greatest version of you.

The Rune of Berkana is said to indicate that we are entering a new phase in life that will leads to a blossoming and ripening and is therefore representative of new beginnings. Its energy is gentle and penetrating and calls us to provide the best possible conditions for something new to emerge.

Be your Brilliant Self

3

Be Great Today... Be Brilliant...
This card asks you to get in touch with the
extraordinariness of everyday living.
Go about your daily life doing everything to the very best
of your ability. Be Extraordinary in an Ordinary way.
Your brilliance will radiate into the world creating more
change than you could possibly imagine.

**Additional messages and guidance.**
This card invites you to become present to the magnificence of the everyday things and the endless opportunities that you have, to
be extraordinary, in an ordinary way.
Each day we say and do a multitude of things, many of which take place on autopilot. Whether you are involved in a simple task such as hanging the washing on the line, or you are engaged in something that is seemingly bigger, such as holding an important meeting or conversation, you are asked to place equal importance in all of your actions and activities, engaging
in everything to the very best of your ability.

**1** Monday
Virgo / Libra

Festivals of Imbolc - Northern Hemisphere and Lammas – Southern Hemisphere

**2** Tuesday
Libra

**3** Wednesday
Libra / Scorpio

**4** Thursday
Scorpio

Last Quarter Moon

**5** Friday
Scorpio / Sagittarius

————————————— Journaling and Notes —————————————

- - - - - - - - - - - - - - - - - - - - - - - - - - - - - - - - - - - - - - - - - - - - - - - - - - - - - - - - - - - - - - -

## 6 Saturday
**Sagittarius**

- - - - - - - - - - - - - - - - - - - - - - - - - - - - - - - - - - - - - - - - - - - - - - - - - - - - - - - - - - - - - - -

## 7 Sunday
**Sagittarius / Capricorn**

**8** Monday
Capricorn

**9** Tuesday
Capricorn

**10** Wednesday
Capricorn / Aquarius

**11** Thursday
Aquarius

New Moon LA 11.05 – NY 14.05 - London 19.05

**12** Friday
Aquarius / Pisces

New Moon NY Sydney 06.05 – Auckland 08.05

**13** Saturday
Pisces

**14** Sunday
Pisces / Aries

Valentine's Day

February 2021

---

**15** Monday
Aries

------------------------------------------------------------

**16** Tuesday
Aries

Daily Collective Prayer Begins – 1 Minute of Silent Prayer 7pm daily until 24<sup>th</sup> February
------------------------------------------------------------

**17** Wednesday
Aries / Taurus

------------------------------------------------------------

**18** Thursday
Taurus

Sun enters Pisces
------------------------------------------------------------

**19** Friday
Taurus / Gemini

First Quarter Moon
------------------------------------------------------------

Journaling and Notes

---

**20** Saturday
**Gemini**

---

**21** Sunday
**Gemini**

**Mercury Retrograde Ends**

**22** Monday
Gemini / Cancer

---

**23** Tuesday
Cancer

---

**24** Wednesday
Cancer / Leo

**Daily Collective Prayer Ends Today – Thank you**

---

**25** Thursday
Leo

---

**26** Friday
Leo / Virgo

---

———————————— Journaling and Notes ————————————

-------------------------------------------------------------------------------------------------

**27** Saturday
Virgo

Full Moon LA 00.17 - NY 03.17 – London 08.17 - Sydney 19.17 - Auckland 21.17
-------------------------------------------------------------------------------------------------

**28** Sunday
Virgo / Libra

# Welcome to March 2021

At last we begin to see a lifting of the intensity of the beginning of this powerful year!

On **the 13<sup>th</sup> March we have a beautiful New Moon in Pisces** aligning with deeply spiritual Neptune, who is also uniting with Venus, the planet of harmony balance, love and relationships. They in turn form a favorable connection with Pluto, the planet of transformation and rebirth.

The energy flow at this New Moon is particularly conducive to enhancing our connection with the divine, enhancing the power to initiate wishes that bring balance, harmony and love into all areas of our lives. Our cards and runes highlight how to best align with this profound energetic opportunity for conscious transformation. Mannaz, the Rune of the Self acknowledges that we ourselves are the source of change in our lives, and the Oracle Card of Allow Yourself to Receive, invites us to take full advantage of the divine guidance that may come our way at this time, especially during our meditation practice.

If you find that the Neptunian energy is bringing such a stream of illumination that you feel slightly swamped by information, simply slow down and **Allow Yourself to Receive**. Absorb it all before reflecting.

As we approach the Equinox on the 20<sup>th</sup>, and the Sun also enters Aries, symbolizing the beginning of a new astrological year, the timing is exceptional for the creation of new beginnings. Should anything in your world require change, then the restructuring influence of Saturn will highlight any adjustments needed.

This dynamic is beautifully acknowledged by **Thurisaz, the Rune of Gateway**, who invites us to pause and take time to review before making any adjustments. **Our second Oracle Card of Course Correct** confirms this energetic flow.

In the two days either side of the equinox the earth pauses for breath before entering a new cycle of growth and evolution, we can often unknowingly tune into this shift and feel a little disorientated. Do not be concerned, all will become clear as we move to **the Full Moon in Libra on the 28<sup>th</sup>** with a stunning flow of harmonious energy highlighting any areas of our lives that need to be brought back into balance.

The Rune of Mannaz, or the Self, invites us to open ourselves to the divine, and acknowledges that we are undergoing a deeply personal and profound personal transition. Remain humble, get still and learn to listen. Remove judgement and open yourself to receive guidance of the highest order.

Allow yourself to Receive

1

One of the greatest blocks in our ability to manifest our
greatest desires is
an inability to allow ourselves to receive.
This card asks that you take some time to identify any
inner beliefs, perceptions and attitudes
that stop you from receiving and one by one,
remove these resistances.

**Additional messages and guidance.**

There are many reasons why we block ourselves from receiving, but one thing is certain, it will almost always go back to some event in our past.

It is understandable to be fearful if we have been hurt or damaged by others, but in trying to shut out bad experiences, we also shut out the good ones too, closing ourselves to the possibility of healing.

It is time to move beyond your fears. Give yourself permission to receive. If this card is drawn in response to a particular person or situation, this card asks you to lower your defense's
and take a risk.

The Rune of Thurisaz, or Gateway, advises us to contemplate. Reflection and Guidance are needed before proceeding. Pause and review. Lean into a space of gratitude for all that you have experienced both good and bad, this has made you who you are today. You are now ready to proceed!

Course Correct

9

If an obstacle or diversion has interrupted your plans, this card is here to assure you that the delay is providential, bringing you an opportunity to pause and reassess in order to fine tune your direction.

Additional messages and guidance.
In our goal driven culture, we so often interpret disruptions, delays and diversions as a negative experience, creating frustration and leaving us feeling angry or helpless. However, if we change our perspective and trust that the universe is bringing us exactly what we need... exactly when we need it... then we can understand that even a delay or diversion is in fact a gift, bringing us a sign or a communication that we need to make some adjustments, course correct, or even take a completely different direction.

This card is here to reassure you that any delays taking place in your current situation are timely and are simply signposts to assist you in taking the next step in the right direction.

**1** Monday
Libra

**2** Tuesday
Libra / Scorpio

**3** Wednesday
Scorpio

**4** Thursday
Scorpio / Sagittarius

**5** Friday
Sagittarius

--------------------- Journaling and Notes ---------------------

**6** Saturday
**Sagittarius**

**Last Quarter Moon**

**7** Sunday
**Sagittarius / Capricorn**

**8** Monday
Capricorn

**9** Tuesday
Capricorn / Aquarius

**10** Wednesday
Aquarius

**11** Thursday
Aquarius / Pisces

**12** Friday
Pisces

Journaling and Notes

**13** Saturday
**Pisces / Aries**

New Moon LA 02.21 – NY 05.21 - London 10.21 - Sydney 21.21 – Auckland 23.21

**14** Sunday
**Aries**

**UK Mother's Day**

**15** Monday
**Aries**

**16** Tuesday
**Aries / Taurus**

**17** Wednesday
**Taurus**

**Ireland St. Patrick's Day**

**18** Thursday
**Taurus / Gemini**

**Sun enters Pisces**

**19** Friday
**Gemini**

──────────── Journaling and Notes ────────────

## 20 Saturday
Gemini

Sun enters Aries
Spring Equinox Northern Hemisphere – Autumn Equinox Southern Hemisphere

## 21 Sunday
Gemini / Cancer

First Quarter Moon

## 22 Monday
Cancer

## 23 Tuesday
Cancer / Leo

## 24 Wednesday
Leo

## 25 Thursday
Leo

## 26 Friday
Leo / Virgo

―――――――――――――――― Journaling and Notes ――――――――――――

―――――――――――――――――――――――――――――――――――――――――――――――――――

## 27 Saturday
Virgo

―――――――――――――――――――――――――――――――――――――――――――――――――――

## 28 Sunday
Virgo / Libra

**UK Clocks Change**
**Full Moon LA 11.48 - NY 14.48 – London 19.48**

# Reflections from March

-------------------------------------------------- Journaling & Notes --------------------------------------------------

68

# Welcome to April 2021

April promises to bring us a huge opportunity to create new beginnings and a fresh start, and in terms of manifestation, aided by the insights and guidance brought to us by our Oracle Cards and Runes, we can consciously navigate the energetics of this month to their fullest potential.

In the first two weeks leading up to **the New Moon in Aries on the 12th** the energy is primed to bring to our awareness any areas of our lives that need to heal. **Our Oracle Card of Independence and Nauthiz, the Rune of Constraint**, invite us to notice any aspects of our lives that are still being influenced by negativity from the past, and to attend to these issues to bring about healing and an opportunity for new beginnings.

Use the energy of **the New Moon in Aries** to focus on any areas of life that fire you up, both the positives and the negatives.

If your passions light up over an injustice in the past, then use your New Moon wishes to reach out for healing. We define our desires as much through those things that we dislike, as those things that we enjoy to the fullest! Rather than dwelling on any negative past experiences in ways that continue to fuel unease and unrest, use your memories of events to create a crystal clear definition of those things that you do wish to manifest and be sure to list these in your top ten wishes alongside any healing that needs to occur to make this possible.

**The Sun enters Taurus on the 19th** and as we journey through the month, the astrology suggests that we may find much being brought to the surface, with the kind of revelations and disclosures that can seem a little shocking at times, however they arrive with purpose, waking us up to those areas of life that are calling for change.

**The Full Moon in Scorpio on the 27th** makes a strong connection with the restructuring energy of Saturn, and Uranus, the bringer of change through disruption! This **Full Moon** firmly requests that we pay attention to all that comes to light. A harmonious flow of energy simultaneously connects our Moon with the dynamic warrior planet of Mars and Jupiter the planet of expansive new opportunities. **Our second Oracle Card of Collaborate and Berkana, the Rune of Growth** request that we embrace new ways of relating with one another, calling for healthy inter-dependent relationships that thrive on the basis of autonomy and respect.

The Rune of Nauthiz suggests that work will be needed to bring about a flow and create a move forward. Journey inwards and remove any blocks from within that may be holding you back. Cross the T's and dot the I's. "When fishermen can't go to sea, they mend their nets!"

Independence

24

Independence is a wonderful attribute, but if taken to an extreme, it can border on isolation. Sometimes if we have been hurt or let down, or trapped in a co-dependent relationship, we lose faith in others and learn only to rely on ourselves. This card calls you to question this inner belief and to develop healthy inter-dependent relationships with an equality of both giving and receiving.

### Additional messages and guidance.

Are you independent to an extreme? If so, re-evaluate your position. Trace the origins of this pattern of behavior back to the source and let go of any defenses' that are holding you back.

Are you an over giver and continually look after others whilst not attending to your own needs? This creates a subtle form of independence. Over giving stops people from being able to give to you! This keeps people at a distance, inadvertently creating a sense of isolated independence. Learn to listen to your own needs and allow yourself to give others the opportunity to give to you.

The Rune of Berkana is an indication that we are entering a new phase in life that will lead to a blossoming and ripening and is therefore representative of new beginnings. Its energy is gentle and penetrating and calls us to provide the best possible conditions for something new to emerge.

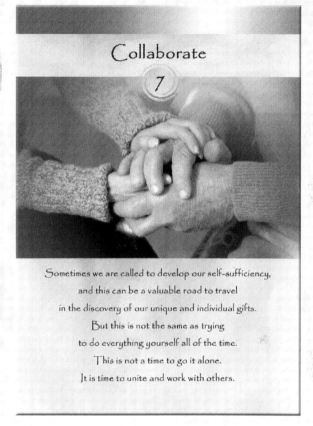

Collaborate

7

Sometimes we are called to develop our self-sufficiency,
and this can be a valuable road to travel
in the discovery of our unique and individual gifts.
But this is not the same as trying
to do everything yourself all of the time.
This is not a time to go it alone.
It is time to unite and work with others.

**Additional messages and guidance.**
If we have ever experienced people letting us down or something not working out as we had hoped it is a natural response to withdraw and as a result, become acutely self-sufficient. However, this is a defensive response, and whilst understandable, it can close us to the possibility of receiving the help and support that we need... and deserve!

This card carries a clear message. It is time to collaborate and to work with others. If this card is drawn in response to a question about a particular person, or a specific group of people, this card is here to reassure you that they are trustworthy.

---

**29** Monday
Libra

Full Moon Sydney 05.48 – Auckland 07.48

---

**30** Tuesday
Libra / Scorpio

---

**31** Wednesday
Scorpio

---

**1** Thursday
Scorpio / Sagittarius

---

**2** Friday
Sagittarius

Good Friday

---

—————————————— Journaling and Notes ——————————————

---

**3** Saturday
**Sagittarius / Capricorn**

---

**4** Sunday
**Capricorn**

**Easter Sunday**
**Last Quarter Moon**

---

**5** Monday
Capricorn / Aquarius

Easter Monday

**6** Tuesday
Aquarius

**7** Wednesday
Aquarius / Pisces

**8** Thursday
Pisces

**9** Friday
Pisces

———————————— Journaling and Notes ————————————

-------------------------------------------------------------------------------

**10** Saturday
**Pisces / Aries**

-------------------------------------------------------------------------------

**11** Sunday
**Aries**

**New Moon LA 19.30 – NY 22.30**
-------------------------------------------------------------------------------

## 12 Monday
**Aries / Taurus**

New Moon London 03.30 - Sydney 12.30 – Auckland 14.30

## 13 Tuesday
**Taurus**

## 14 Wednesday
**Taurus**

## 15 Thursday
**Taurus / Gemini**

## 16 Friday
**Gemini**

**17** Saturday
Gemini / Cancer

Sun enters Aries
Spring Equinox Northern Hemisphere – Autumn Equinox Southern Hemisphere

**18** Sunday
Cancer

## 19 Monday
Cancer

Sun enters Taurus

## 20 Tuesday
Cancer / Leo

First Quarter Moon

## 21 Wednesday
Leo

## 22 Thursday
Leo / Virgo

## 23 Friday
Virgo

———————————————— Journaling and Notes ————————————————

--------------------------------------------------------------------------------

**24** Saturday
**Virgo / Libra**

--------------------------------------------------------------------------------

**25** Sunday
**Libra**

# Reflections from April

-------------------------------------------------- Journaling & Notes --------------------------------------------------

# Welcome to May 2021

As we journey through this profoundly transformative year of 2021, the month of May continues to highlight any areas of tension between the old and the new with an invitation to embrace the changes that will carry humanity into a new dawn and a new age.

**Our Oracle Cards of Empower Yourself and Collaborate**, embody the energy of the month, highlighting the natural tension that sits between the needs and desires of an individual, versus the needs of the greater collective; and the needs and desires of humanity, versus the needs of our beautiful planet.

Showing up for a second month in a row, **the card of Collaborate** reinforces the message, it is time to work together! It is time to understand the nature of true personal empowerment and how to integrate this with the empowerment of a collective and unified vision for a united future.

**The New Moon in Taurus on the 11th** makes a flowing connection with Pluto, enhancing our transformative capabilities. Saturn and the North Node bring a strong Karmic influence, and with input from Chiron, the creator of the rainbow bridge, said to support humanity through the transition into a new age of higher consciousness, the energy of this new moon invites us to sow seeds and set wishes that honor our spiritual connectivity and relationship with all of life.

**Our Runes this month of Inguz, the Rune of Fertility and Gebo, the Rune of Partnership** align beautifully with the energetic of **the Sun entering Gemini on the 20th**, reinforcing the need to hold a collective vision that can initiate new beginnings. **A rune of great power, the Rune of Fertility** requires the completion of the beginning phase of something and brings us the energy that we need in order to find clarify and seek resolutions, **whilst the Rune of partnership** calls us not to collapse into the highs and lows of emotional intensity within relationship.

Now in the shadow period of **the 29th May Mercury Retrograde**, if a delay or hold up occurs, trust that this will have purpose, even if we cannot yet see the bigger picture. With the Uranus and Saturn connection intensifying, when we reach **the Full Moon Eclipse in Sagittarius on the 27th**, we can expect powerful portals of energetic changes that align us with the true essence of what it means to be a Spiritual Warrior.

The Rune of Inguz speaks of new beginnings and the urge to bring harmony into our relationships. It calls for the completion of beginnings and invites us to find solutions and resolutions that will free us to embark on the new. This powerful Rune heralds a period of emergence and fertility.

Empower Yourself

14

Empowerment does not mean that we have power over others, it means that we have Power over ourselves. We honour our capacity for Free Will and Conscious Choice whilst honouring the same in others. This card asks you to evaluate your present situation and to take an ownership of your right to choose, with a recognition of the entitlement of others to do the same.

**Additional messages and guidance.**
This card brings a clear message. Please review your present situation and take full ownership of your personal entitlement to choose the direction that is right for you.

If your question is in response to a relationship issue, it may be that you are tangled in some sort of power struggle within that relationship. If so, you are asked to hold firm in your own entitlement to choose, however please also recognize that the other person may hold a completely different perspective and may desire and indeed choose a different direction, one that is appropriate for their journey at this moment in time.

The Rune of Gebo informs us that the energy of partnership is around us and calls us to unite, whilst simultaneously recognizing and valuing our unique individual pathways. Fundamentally, this Rune calls for equality in every aspect of relationship, not only with other humans, but with all of life.

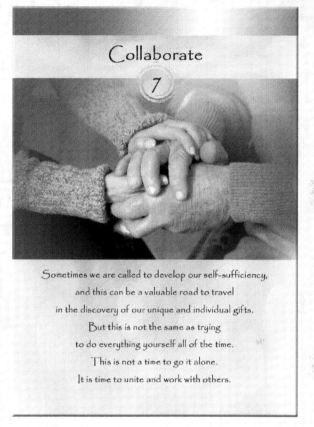

Collaborate

7

Sometimes we are called to develop our self-sufficiency,
and this can be a valuable road to travel
in the discovery of our unique and individual gifts.
But this is not the same as trying
to do everything yourself all of the time.
This is not a time to go it alone.
It is time to unite and work with others.

### Additional messages and guidance.
If we have ever experienced people letting us down or something not working out as we had hoped it is a natural response to withdraw and as a result, become acutely self-sufficient. However, this is a defensive response, and whilst understandable, it can close us to the possibility of receiving the help and support that we need... and deserve!

This card carries a clear message. It is time to collaborate and to work with others. If this card is drawn in response to a question about a particular person, or a specific group of people, this card is here to reassure you that they are trustworthy.

**26** Monday
Libra / Scorpio

Super Full Moon LA 20.31 – NY 23.31

**27** Tuesday
Scorpio

Super Full Moon London 04.31 - Sydney 13.31 – Auckland 15.31

**28** Wednesday
Scorpio / Sagittarius

**29** Thursday
Sagittarius

**30** Friday
Sagittarius / Capricorn

**1** Saturday
Capricorn

Festival of Beltane Northern Hemisphere – Samhain Southern Hemisphere

**2** Sunday
Capricorn / Aquarius

**3** Monday
**Aquarius**

UK Early May Bank Holiday
Last Quarter Moon

**4** Tuesday
**Aquarius**

**5** Wednesday
**Aquarius / Pisces**

**6** Thursday
**Pisces**

**7** Friday
**Pisces / Aries**

—————————— Journaling and Notes ——————————

-------------------------------------------------------------------------------

**8** Saturday
**Aries**

-------------------------------------------------------------------------------

**9** Sunday
**Aries / Taurus**

**USA, Australia & New Zealand Mother's Day**
-------------------------------------------------------------------------------

**10** Monday
Taurus

**11** Tuesday
Taurus

New Moon LA 11.59 – NY 14.59 - London 19.59

**12** Wednesday
Taurus / Gemini

New Moon Sydney 04.59 – Auckland 06.59

**13** Thursday
Gemini

**14** Friday
Gemini

**15** Saturday
Gemini / Cancer

**16** Sunday
Cancer

**17** Monday
Cancer / Leo

**18** Tuesday
Leo

**19** Wednesday
Leo / Virgo

First Quarter Moon

**20** Thursday
Virgo

Sun enters Gemini

**21** Friday
Virgo

-------------------------------------------------------------------------------------------

**22** Saturday
Virgo / Libra

-------------------------------------------------------------------------------------------

**23** Sunday
Libra

**24** Monday
Libra / Scorpio

**25** Tuesday
Scorpio

**26** Wednesday
Scorpio / Sagittarius

Full Moon Eclipse LA 04.13 – NY 07.13 - London 12.13 - Sydney 21.13 – Auckland 23.13

**27** Thursday
Sagittarius

**28** Friday
Sagittarius / Capricorn

Journaling and Notes

---

**29** Saturday
**Capricorn**

**Mercury in Retrograde until 22nd June**

---

**30** Sunday
**Capricorn / Aquarius**

# Welcome to June 2021

June looks to bring a culmination of energetics that create a pivotal turning point in a year of profound transformation. **Following the New Moon Eclipse on the 10th, the intensity of the Uranus and Saturn connection peaks on the 14th and with Mercury in retrograde until the 22nd** we can expect potential delays and sudden events that declare and confirm that an old era has come to an end and we must now embark wholeheartedly on the pathway of the new.

**Our Oracle Cards of Problems and The Spiritual Warrior** align perfectly with this energetic of transformation through awareness, self-responsibility and self-empowerment. **The card of Problems** requests that we perceive a problem as an opportunity and from within that space of awareness, seek the solution. **This card sits with the Blank Rune** which symbolizes both an end and a beginning and a pivotal turning point when the new is about to emerge. **The card of the Spiritual** Warrior urges us to take only right action, and in aligning with Kano, the Rune of Openings, suggests that we are ready to move from darkness into light and that our pathway will become clear.

The energetics of the New Moon Eclipse are varied and dynamic. With the Moon linking favorably with Saturn, our desires for restructuring are supported, however with Saturn intensely connected to Uranus, the bringer of sudden revolutionary change, additional input from transformational Pluto and fiery Mars, and a less harmonious connection with watery Neptune we may feel pressure to act and yet confused as to which way to go. Try to take some time out, meditate, and open yourself to receive higher guidance.

**On the 21st June on the Solstice the Sun enters Cancer and with Mercury stationing direct on the 22nd** the timing is perfect for us to receive the guidance we need to find clarity and renewed direction. Open yourself to receive. It is highly likely under the current astro-influences that the answers you seek may be unconventional and come from unexpected sources.

The energetics of **the Full Moon in Capricorn on the 24th** are an interesting mix, calling for gentle, mindful responsiveness and yet simultaneously urging us to take action. If any circumstances in your world are calling to be changed, embrace the changes with optimism and take the steps you are shown. This pivotal month asks us to embrace the changes we are shown, believe in in new and better future, and lean into a space of trust.

The Blank Rune is both an end and a beginning and represented the unknowable future. Like the phoenix rising from the ashes, it is associated with fate and destiny and is a symbolic acknowledgement that some way of living is naturally and appropriately coming to an end.

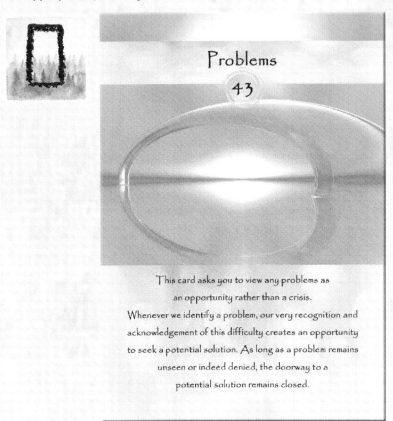

Problems

43

This card asks you to view any problems as an opportunity rather than a crisis.
Whenever we identify a problem, our very recognition and acknowledgement of this difficulty creates an opportunity to seek a potential solution. As long as a problem remains unseen or indeed denied, the doorway to a potential solution remains closed.

**Additional messages and guidance.**
When we perceive a problem as a crisis, we immediately load it with highly charged emotions that fuel uncertainty, anxiety and fears of being unable to find a resolution. In truth, until a problem can be openly identified, the solution and way forwards will remain hidden and unavailable to us.

Whatever problems you are facing, you are asked to adjust your perspective to one of positivity in which your mind becomes open and available to receive the guidance that you need in order to progress and find a resolution.

The Rune of Kano speaks of renewed clarity, and a dispelling of darkness whilst acknowledging that we ourselves are the source of change in our lives. It indicates that we will be shown aspects of our lives that were previously hidden from view and the actions needed to initiate the new.

# The Spiritual Warrior

The Pathway of the Spiritual Warrior
and the Calling of your Soul.

**Additional messages and guidance.**
Sometimes this card indicates a series of events/circumstances/situations that have created a gradual awakening within you, causing you to question your current circumstances. Sometimes it can indicate a sudden, out of your control event, that has pushed you to have to make decisions and change course or you may have been feeling restless and as if something needs to change. Perhaps you are already in the process of a major transition in your life and wondering if you have taken the right direction.

Whatever your situation, this card is an affirmation. You are invited to listen to your circumstances as a form of guidance. You are aligning with the calling of your Soul. This is the pathway of the Spiritual Warrior.

**31** Monday
Aquarius

UK Spring Bank Holiday

**1** Tuesday
Aquarius / Pisces

**2** Wednesday
Pisces

Last Quarter Moon

**3** Thursday
Pisces / Aries

**4** Friday
Aries

———————————— Journaling and Notes ————————————

-----------------------------------------------------------------------------

**5** Saturday
Aries

-----------------------------------------------------------------------------

**6** Sunday
Aries / Taurus

**7** Monday
Taurus

**8** Tuesday
Taurus / Gemini

**9** Wednesday
Gemini

**10** Thursday
Gemini

New Moon Eclipse LA 03.52 – NY 06.52 – London 11.52 - Sydney 20.52 – Auckland 22.52

**11** Friday
Gemini / Cancer

———————————————— Journaling and Notes ————————————————

**12** Saturday
Cancer

**13** Sunday
Cancer / Leo

**Daily Collective Prayer Begins – 1 Minute of Silent Prayer 7pm daily until 7<sup>th</sup> June**

**14** Monday
Leo

**15** Tuesday
Leo

**16** Wednesday
Leo / Virgo

**17** Thursday
Virgo

Daily Collective Prayer Ends Today – Thank you

**18** Friday
Virgo / Libra

First Quarter Moon

———————————— Journaling and Notes ————————————

-------------------------------------------------------------------------------

**19** Saturday
Libra

-------------------------------------------------------------------------------

**20** Sunday
Libra / Scorpio

**UK & USA Father's Day**

## 21 Monday
Scorpio

Sun enters Cancer
Summer Solstice Northern Hemisphere – Winter Solstice Southern Hemisphere

## 22 Tuesday
Scorpio / Sagittarius

Mercury Retrograde Ends

## 23 Wednesday
Sagittarius

## 24 Thursday
Sagittarius / Capricorn

Full Moon LA 11.39 – NY 14.39 - London 19.39

## 25 Friday
Capricorn

Full Moon Sydney 04.39 – Auckland 06.39

## 26 Saturday
**Capricorn / Aquarius**

## 27 Sunday
**Aquarius**

---------------------------------------------- Journaling & Notes ----------------------------------------------

# Welcome to July 2021

The tension between Uranus and Saturn continues into July, establishing a strong connection with the masculine and feminine warrior planets of Mars and Venus. With Pluto, Saturn, Jupiter and Neptune all now in retrograde we can expect a tension between the desire to move forwards and initiate the new, versus the challenges that we face in finding a comprehensive way forwards along with a certain degree of resistance to change.

The energetics of **the New Moon in Cancer on the 10th** invites potential illumination, although these insights may not necessarily flow into our lives with ease. **Our first Oracle Card of Miracles** reminds us that even challenges and uncertainty can after the event be seen and understood to have been a miracle, bringing us exactly what we needed to proceed. **Aligning with Sowelu, the Rune of Wholeness**, we are asked to center ourselves in the knowledge that ultimately, the universe will always have the upper hand.

Sometimes we need to get out of our own way and **our second Rune, Dagaz, the Rune of Breakthrough**, suggests that clarity will emerge, even if unexpectedly, and that significant changes may be called for. For some this Rune signifies moving in an entirely new direction. **The Card of Choices and Decisions** asks us not to be afraid of making the wrong choice and to center ourselves in the knowledge that however we proceed, we will always learn from any situation and can always change course again if needed.

Whilst the union of Mars and Venus, exact on the 13th, asks us not to engage in battles of power and to strive for solutions that honor equality and validate the needs of all parties, **as the Sun enters Leo on the 22nd** and the energy builds **to the Full Moon in Aquarius on the 24th**, we see a tension between Pluto, the planet of re-birth and transformation, now in retrograde and Mercury, the great communicator. I am delighted to say that this connection is softened by the higher spiritual energy of Neptune, and so if any negotiations were previously at a stalemate and going nowhere, there is now an opportunity to birth decisive and clear solutions that come from a higher perspective.

The Rune of Sowelu embodies wholeness and is an indication of the path that we must follow. This Rune symbolizes transformation and regeneration right down to a cellular level. A Rune of great power it brings us the life force and energy to undertake this process of transformation.

# MIRACLES
## 33

We tend to perceive miracles only when our personal
desires are met, and yet when we look back,
almost all of us will be able to recall a crisis or a challenge
that ultimately proved to be a miraculous turning point
and an extraordinary gift.
This card asks you to see the miracles that surround you
right now and in every situation.

**Additional messages and guidance.**
This card is a challenge to shift your perspective of the meaning of the word Miracle. We are surrounded by miracles every day, but to appreciate them in their fullest, we must shift our perspective to one of an openness that stretches beyond any ego centered desires and recognize that greater forces are in motion.

If you are facing challenges in your life this card calls you to recognize that miracles come in many different shapes and sizes. There is a greater plan and even though you may not be able to see your part in it at this present moment, this card comes as reassurance that everything is taking place just as it should and you will soon be able to see the miracles that are being sent to guide you.

The Rune of Dagaz is said to signal a major shift and transformation. If we embrace this energy and rise to the challenge this rune validates that the outcome is assured but also states that it may not come in the form that we expect. This rune heralds a major turning point!

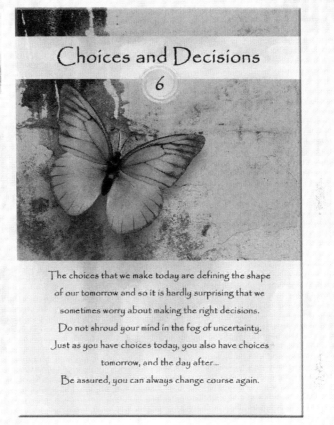

Choices and Decisions

6

The choices that we make today are defining the shape
of our tomorrow and so it is hardly surprising that we
sometimes worry about making the right decisions.
Do not shroud your mind in the fog of uncertainty.
Just as you have choices today, you also have choices
tomorrow, and the day after...
Be assured, you can always change course again.

**Additional messages and guidance.**
Do you overburden yourself in the process of making decisions, creating an internal stream of thoughts that try to anticipate every potential outcome for fear of making the wrong choice?

In truth, there is no such thing as a wrong choice or a wrong decision. None of us can actually know how something will be until we get there and try it on for size! This is how we learn and grow and discover the things that work for us, as well as the things that do not, helping us to find clarity in our future decisions and choices. An essential part of the process of manifestation.

**28** Monday
**Aquarius / Pisces**

**29** Tuesday
**Pisces**

**30** Wednesday
**Pisces**

**1** Thursday
**Pisces / Aries**

**Last Quarter Moon**

**2** Friday
**Aries**

———————————— Journaling and Notes ————————————

---

**3** Saturday
**Aries / Taurus**

---

**4** Sunday
**Taurus**

**USA Independence Day**

---

**5** Monday
Taurus

USA Independence Day Holiday

-------------------------------------------------------------------

**6** Tuesday
Taurus / Gemini

-------------------------------------------------------------------

**7** Wednesday
Gemini

-------------------------------------------------------------------

**8** Thursday
Gemini / Cancer

-------------------------------------------------------------------

**9** Friday
Cancer

New Moon LA 18.16 – NY 21.16

-------------------------------------------------------------------

—————————— Journaling and Notes ——————————

-------------------------------------------------------------------------------

**10** Saturday
Cancer

New Moon London 02.16 – Sydney 11.16 – Auckland 13.16
-------------------------------------------------------------------------------

**11** Sunday
Cancer / Leo

**12** Monday
Leo

**13** Tuesday
Leo / Virgo

**14** Wednesday
Virgo

**15** Thursday
Virgo / Libra

**16** Friday
Libra

Journaling and Notes

**17** Saturday
Libra / Scorpio

**First Quarter Moon**

**18** Sunday
Scorpio

**19** Monday
Scorpio / Sagittarius

**20** Tuesday
Sagittarius

**21** Wednesday
Sagittarius / Capricorn

**22** Thursday
Capricorn

Sun enters Leo

**23** Friday
Capricorn

Full Moon LA 19.36 – NY 22.36

———————————— Journaling and Notes ————————————

---

**24** Saturday
**Capricorn / Aquarius**

**Full Moon London 03.36 - Sydney 12.36 – Auckland 14.36**

---

**25** Sunday
**Aquarius**

---

**26** Monday
Aquarius / Pisces

---

**27** Tuesday
Pisces

---

**28** Wednesday
Pisces / Aries

---

**29** Thursday
Aries

---

**30** Friday
Aries / Taurus

---

———————————— Journaling and Notes ————————————

---

**31** Saturday
Taurus

**Last Quarter Moon**

---

**1** Sunday
Taurus

Festival of Lammas Northern Hemisphere – Imbolc Southern Hemisphere

# Reflections from July

----------------------------------------- Journaling & Notes -----------------------------------------

# Welcome to August 2021

In a month that supports action and productivity, **the New Moon in Leo on the 8th** invites us to set wishes and intentions that unite the needs of the individual with those of the greater collective. In a year when so much has been systematically revealed to us, it is time to pull the information together and build a blueprint for the future. With both Venus and Mars progressing through Virgo, during the month of August we are asked not only to dream of the world that we wish to see, but also to take actions to initiate the process of manifesting this dream into reality.

**Mercury, the winged messenger of the Gods, enters Virgo on the 12th,** journeying to meet with Mars, exact on the 19th. This collaboration invites us to enter into the kinds of conversations that can transform ideas into actions. **Our first Oracle Card of Have Your Voice and Ehwaz, the Rune of Movement**, suggest the bettering of any situation and of the potential for situations to gather momentum through helpful and productive conversation.

**Our second Oracle Card of Grace** harmonizes with Venus as she moves into Libra on the 17th bringing balance to the diminishing connection between Saturn and Uranus that has been demanding radical change. **Our second Rune, Jera, the Rune of Harvest** indicates a new cycle of growth and calls us to cultivate with care, reminding us that nurture is required to bring the new to a stage of fruition and harvest. Any changes that we initiate during this time on the basis of universal love have the potential to flow into being with ease. This is a busy month that lends itself well to productivity, especially in sowing seeds for the new and in the name of love.

A Full Moon will always illuminate that which we need to see in order to make adjustments, course correct, or indeed simply to validate that we are either on track... or not! **The Full Moon in Aquarius on the 22nd**, just 9 hours before **the Sun enters Virgo**, brings vibrant and flowing energy to any of the ideas that we placed into our New Moon wishing lists earlier in the month and have subsequently taken actions to put into motion. This full Moon promises an unusually flowing energetic that can potentially support us in moving something forwards. With Mars and Mercury connecting favorably with Uranus, now in retrograde, we might experience sudden breakthrough moments that call us to re-evaluate, indicating the next steps we need to take to progress.

The Rune of Ehwaz is a Rune of transition and movement and suggests the bettering of any situation. This Rune looks ahead to the future and indicates progress and a gradual moving forwards that will gather momentum and is worthy of our investment.

Have Your Voice

(22)

Is there something that you need to say!
An inability to speak out can leave us with feelings
of hurt and resentment which then create
a kind of internal energetic roadblock.
Voice your feelings to yourself or write them down.
It is time to release the past.

**Additional messages and guidance.**
This card is an indication that you have been unable to voice your true feelings, either directly to a particular person or you have been unable to speak openly about a situation.

Even if other people around you are unable to listen to you, it is still important for you to have a voice. You may wish to write a "Not to Send" letter. Write about your situation stating exactly how you feel and why you feel that way, then either bury the letter or burn it and allow the winds of heaven to take it away, along with any emotional residue that had remained.

The Rune of Jera speaks of beneficial outcomes, however it also acknowledges that continued work and dedication are needed to bring our ideas or project into fruition. This Rune requests commitment and patience suggesting a full year is needed to complete the cycle of manifestation.

GRACE
20

When we sit in relationship with Grace, we see every situation through the eyes of love, fostering our desire to meet life with understanding, compassion and kindness. This card asks that you view your situation with Grace.
Will Understanding bring Compassion?
How would Love view your possible choices?
What would Kindness suggest that you do?

### Additional messages and guidance.

Grace is that extraordinary voice within us that supports us in approaching all aspects of our lives with harmony, balance, love and kindness, always desiring to give the very best of ourselves in any situation, even if we find ourselves in a conflictual situation or needing to do something that we would perhaps rather not do.

When Grace flows through us, love becomes the focus of all of our thoughts, words and actions, radiating out into the world, positively affecting everyone and everything we come into contact with. If this card is drawn in response to a challenging situation or person, you are asked to stand back and review your situation through the eyes of grace. Now take action accordingly.

# August 2021

**2** Monday
Taurus / Gemini

**3** Tuesday
Gemini

**4** Wednesday
Gemini / Cancer

**5** Thursday
Cancer

**6** Friday
Cancer

──────────────── Journaling and Notes ────────────────

**7** Saturday
Cancer / Leo

**8** Sunday
Leo

New Moon LA 06.50 – NY 09.50 - London 14.50 – Sydney 23.50

**9** Monday
Leo / Virgo

New Moon Auckland 01.50

**10** Tuesday
Virgo

**11** Wednesday
Virgo / Libra

**12** Thursday
Libra

**13** Friday
Libra

———————————— Journaling and Notes ————————————

**14** Saturday
Libra / Scorpio

**15** Sunday
Scorpio

First Quarter Moon

**16** Monday
Scorpio / Sagittarius

**17** Tuesday
Sagittarius

**18** Wednesday
Sagittarius / Capricorn

**19** Thursday
Capricorn

**20** Friday
Capricorn / Aquarius

——————————— Journaling and Notes ———————————

**21** Saturday
Aquarius

-------------------------------------------------------------------------------

**22** Sunday
Aquarius / Pisces

Sun enters Virgo
Full Moon LA 05.02 – NY 08.01 - London 13.01 - Sydney 22.01

-------------------------------------------------------------------------------

## **23** Monday
Pisces

Full Moon Auckland 00.01

## **24** Tuesday
Pisces / Aries

## **25** Wednesday
Aries

## **26** Thursday
Aries

## **27** Friday
Aries / Taurus

─────────────── Journaling and Notes ───────────────

## **28** Saturday
**Taurus**

## **29** Sunday
**Taurus / Gemini**

-------------------------------------------- Journaling & Notes --------------------------------------------

# Welcome to September 2021

In a year of tough realizations, September seems to offer an opportunity to pause for breath and truly realign in ways that set a new compass for the future. With five of our major planets in retrograde, the energy this month naturally invites us to review, **and our Runes of Thurisaz, the Rune of Gateway, and Othila, the Rune of Separation**, beautifully validate this energetic. **Thurisaz asks us to pause**, to review the past and to evaluate, before stepping through the gateway into the new, whilst **Othila, tells us that we have outgrown something** and brings a clear message that it is time to let go of the past and emerge anew.

Calling us to listen with our hearts rather than our minds **the New Moon in Virgo on the 7<sup>th</sup>** finds an exact and flowing connection with Uranus, the bringer of revolutionary ideas and thinking out of the box solutions. If something unusual or unexpected is revealed, listen and trust that you are being shown what you need to see, to liberate you from past limitations. **Our first Oracle Card of Believe in Yourself** requests that we let go of any negative perceptions that are holding us back, and remember, **a Virgo New Moon** is perfect for setting wishes that release the inner critic.

The incredibly positive energetics of this **New Moon** sees balanced Venus in harmonious relationship with expansive Jupiter, passionate Mars in harmonious relationship with transformative Pluto, and the winged messenger Mercury, in harmonious relationship with karmic Saturn. This is an extraordinarily powerful New moon to set wishes and intentions that value your wellbeing and a healthy life work balance, bringing harmony to all areas of your life.

**When we reach the Full Moon in Pisces on the 20<sup>th</sup>**, messenger Mercury squares up to Pluto, who in turn aligns favorably with the Moon, Sun, Neptune and Mars. **Our Oracle Card of Persevere** reminds us not to be knocked off balance if something unexpected takes place. As Mercury prepares for retrograde on the 27<sup>th</sup>, if a truth is revealed, trust that it needed to be heard and comes with purpose. **On the 22<sup>nd</sup> September we reach the Equinox, and the Sun moves into Libra.** At the equinoxes and Solstices, the Earth pauses for breath. (See page 28 for more details on how best to use the equinox energy.) Use this time for deep meditation and open yourself to any form of healing that brings balance back into your life.

The Rune of Thurisaz, or Gateway, advises us to contemplate. Reflection and Guidance are needed before proceeding. Pause and review. Lean into a space of gratitude for all that you have experienced both good and bad, this has made you who you are today. You are now ready to proceed!

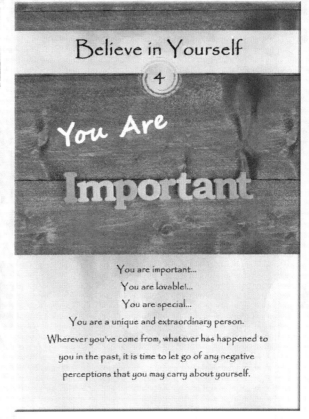

Believe in Yourself

4

You Are

Important

You are important...
You are lovable!...
You are special...
You are a unique and extraordinary person.
Wherever you've come from, whatever has happened to you in the past, it is time to let go of any negative perceptions that you may carry about yourself.

**Additional messages and guidance.**
Low self-esteem is far more common than you might believe. A great many people struggle to believe in themselves, holding deep seated negative or limiting beliefs about themselves. These perspectives stem from earlier experiences, usually in childhood.

If you have faced difficulties in your formative years then this is completely understandable, however it is essential in adult life that we challenge these inner beliefs and empower ourselves to move beyond these limitations.

Let go of any negative perceptions that you may carry about yourself and if necessary, seek counselling or coaching to support you in this process.

The Rune of Othila speaks of separation and acknowledges the rightness of this at this moment in time. Like a snake shedding its skin, we have grown out of a particular situation, some circumstance, or way of being. The separation needed is essential for our long-term growth and benefit.

# PERSEVERE
## 42

Who would have thought that a humble acorn
could grow into a mighty oak tree?
But of course, this takes time. Whatever you are involved
in, this card brings a message of reassurance.
Your hard work and continued effort and dedication
will come to fruition.
You are asked to Persevere and Trust.

**Additional messages and guidance.**
This card is an indication that you have sown seeds that contain powerful long-term possibilities. Whatever it is that you are manifesting and generating within your world, you are asked to persevere, to trust and to believe.

This card honors your diligence and the time and the effort and the hard work that you have been investing, and comes to reassure you that the foundation stones you have been laying for a long-term future will come to fruition, even though further work and perseverance are required.

Have patience and continue on your pathway, one step at a time.

**30** Monday
Gemini

UK Summer Bank Holiday
Last Quarter Moon

**31** Tuesday
Gemini

**1** Wednesday
Gemini / Cancer

**2** Thursday
Cancer

**3** Friday
Cancer / Leo

———————————— Journaling and Notes ————————————

-------------------------------------------------------------------------------------

**4** Saturday
Leo

-------------------------------------------------------------------------------------

**5** Sunday
**Leo / Virgo**

**Australia & New Zealand Father's Day**
-------------------------------------------------------------------------------------

## 6 Monday
Virgo

New Moon LA 17.51 – NY 20.51

## 7 Tuesday
Virgo

New Moon London 01.51 – Sydney 10.51 - Auckland 12.51

## 8 Wednesday
Virgo / Libra

## 9 Thursday
Libra

## 10 Friday
Libra / Scorpio

—————————— Journaling and Notes ——————————

---

## 11 Saturday
**Scorpio**

---

## 12 Sunday
**Scorpio / Sagittarius**

**13** Monday
Sagittarius

First Quarter Moon

**14** Tuesday
Sagittarius / Capricorn

**15** Wednesday
Capricorn

**16** Thursday
Capricorn / Aquarius

**17** Friday
Aquarius

**18** Saturday
**Aquarius / Pisces**

**19** Sunday
**Pisces**

---

**20** Monday
Pisces

Full Moon LA 16.54 – NY 19.54

-------------------------------------------------------------------------------

**21** Tuesday
Pisces / Aries

Full Moon London 00.54 - Sydney 09.54 – Auckland 11.54

-------------------------------------------------------------------------------

**22** Wednesday
Aries

Sun enters Libra
Autumn Equinox Northern Hemisphere – Spring Equinox Southern Hemisphere

-------------------------------------------------------------------------------

**23** Thursday
Aries / Taurus

-------------------------------------------------------------------------------

**24** Friday
Taurus

-------------------------------------------------------------------------------

———————————————— Journaling and Notes ————————————————

---

## **25** Saturday
**Taurus**

---

## **26** Sunday
**Taurus / Gemini**

# Reflections from September

# Welcome to October 2021

As we move into October the incoming astro-energy naturally extends the reflective processes brought to us during September. **Inguz, the Rune of Fertility offers promise**, and yet also requests that we bring some aspect of our lives to a completion in order to clear the way for the new. Sitting with **our first Oracle Card of Don't Wobble**, if September has left you unsure about your choices and decisions then give yourself permission to slow down, and in the name of manifestation, get grounded and use the powerful energetics of **the New Moon in Libra on the 6th** to get focused before placing your wishes and desires into the universe.

As the month progresses the energy builds to an intense **Full Moon in Aries on the 20th**. Expect passions to be ignited and emotions to run high! **This Full Moon is a true calling to the Spiritual Warriors of the earth.** Get grounded; channel and harness the energy into mindful thoughts and actions that keep your thoughts, words and actions rooted in a vision of the greater whole.

**Our second Oracle Card this month of Ground Yourself speaks clearly to us and aligning with Isa, the Rune of Standstill or Ice**, carries a duality of meaning that beautifully aligns with the power of this Full Moon.

On the one hand, **the Rune of Isa** can suggest frustrations at not being able to progress, however it can also call us to slow down. **Tuning in with Inguz, the Rune of Fertility** that requires completion of beginnings, this collaboration invites us to mindfully and thoughtfully take time to notice and bring to our awareness any blocks from within that may be halting or contributing to the delay of our progress, both individually and collectively. It is only through noticing that we can systematically and thoughtfully remove these blocks enabling the ice to melt, re-energizing a flow of movement forwards.

**With structured Saturn and Uranus, the bringer of sudden changes, prepare for their final meeting with expansive Jupiter and transformational Pluto in early November, and the Sun enters Scorpio on the 23rd**, we will be given an opportunity to dive deep within and remove any blocks that have previously been holding us back on our personal journey of manifestation.

The Rune of Inguz speaks of new beginnings and the urge to bring harmony into our relationships. It calls for the completion of beginnings and invites us to find solutions and resolutions that will free us to embark on the new. This powerful Rune heralds a period of emergence and fertility.

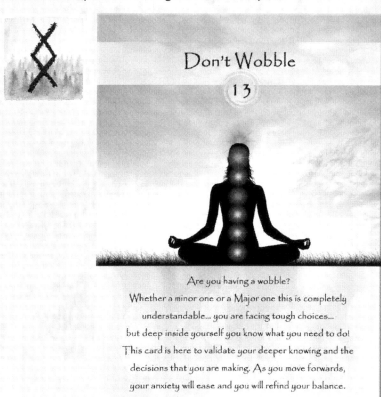

Don't Wobble

13

Are you having a wobble?
Whether a minor one or a Major one this is completely
understandable... you are facing tough choices...
but deep inside yourself you know what you need to do!
This card is here to validate your deeper knowing and the
decisions that you are making. As you move forwards,
your anxiety will ease and you will refind your balance.

**Additional messages and guidance.**
This card brings a clear message. You are facing tough choices that are raising your levels of anxiety. Whatever your situation, this card is here to validate the decisions and the choices that you are making. You know that something has to change, and deep down you know what you need to do.

It is time to take action.

Find a form of meditation that works for you. Either traditional meditation, or perhaps a walking meditation, where you connect with nature. Whatever you do, take time every day to center yourself, to get still, and to connect with the support of the universe that surrounds you. Let go of any self-doubt and trust your inner knowing.

The Rune of Isa speaks of standstill and progress halted, a time when events beyond our control seem to hold us back. However, this Rune also reminds us that are not without power. It advises us to shed, release and cleanse. Releasing the old will make way for the new and bring on the thaw.

Ground Yourself

(21)

This card is a request to you to literally
"Ground Yourself"
Go outdoors, take off your shoes and find somewhere
where it is safe to stand barefoot.
Imagine roots growing out of your feet travelling down
into the soil beneath you, anchoring you with the
nurturing energy of the earth.

## Additional messages and guidance.

Are you struggling to feel grounded or centered? Has a life event thrown you a curve ball, leaving you feeling as though there is no solid ground beneath you? At any given time during the course of our lives, events can take place that leave us feeling vulnerable, wobbly and out of balance.

This card asks you to literally ground yourself. Find somewhere where you can reconnect with nature, even in a city there are always places where you can go. If you are unable to get your bare feet onto the ground, then find a tree in the street and ask it if you may sit with it for a while. You will hear the answer clearly. Or perhaps literally put your hands into some soil. One way or the other you are asked to plug yourself into the energy of the Earth.

# September / October 2021

---

**27** Monday
Gemini

Mercury in Retrograde until 18th October

---

**28** Tuesday
Gemini / Cancer

---

**29** Wednesday
Cancer

Last Quarter Moon

---

**30** Thursday
Cancer

---

**1** Friday
Cancer / Leo

---

———————————— Journaling and Notes ————————————

---

**2** Saturday
Leo

---

**3** Sunday
Leo / Virgo

---

**4** Monday
Virgo

---

**5** Tuesday
Virgo / Libra

---

**6** Wednesday
Libra

New Moon LA 04.05 – NY 07.05 - London 12.05 – Sydney 22.05

---

**7** Thursday
Libra / Scorpio

New Moon Auckland 00.05

---

**8** Friday
Scorpio

——————————————— Journaling and Notes ———————————————

---

**9** Saturday
**Scorpio / Sagittarius**

---

**10** Sunday
**Sagittarius**

**11** Monday
Sagittarius / Capricorn

**12** Tuesday
Capricorn

**13** Wednesday
Capricorn / Aquarius

First Quarter Moon

**14** Thursday
Aquarius

**15** Friday
Aquarius

———————————— Journaling and Notes ————————————

---

## **16** Saturday
**Aquarius / Pisces**

---

## **17** Sunday
**Pisces**

---

---

## 18 Monday
Pisces / Aries

Mercury Retrograde Ends

-------------------------------------------------------------------------

## 19 Tuesday
Aries

Full Moon London 00.54 - Sydney 09.54 – Auckland 11.54

-------------------------------------------------------------------------

## 20 Wednesday
Aries / Taurus

Full Moon LA 07.56 – NY 10.56 – London 15.56

-------------------------------------------------------------------------

## 21 Thursday
Taurus

Full Moon Sydney 01.56 – Auckland 03.56

-------------------------------------------------------------------------

## 22 Friday
Taurus

———————————— Journaling and Notes ————————————

---

**23** Saturday
Taurus / Gemini

**Sun enters Scorpio**

---

**24** Sunday
Gemini

October 2021

**25** Monday
Gemini / Cancer

**26** Tuesday
Cancer

**27** Wednesday
Cancer

**28** Thursday
Cancer / Leo

Last Quarter Moon

**29** Friday
Leo

——————————— Journaling and Notes ———————————

------------------------------------------------------------

**30** Saturday
Leo / Virgo

------------------------------------------------------------

**31** Sunday
Virgo

UK Clocks Change
**Festival of Samhain Northern Hemisphere – Beltane Southern Hemisphere**

------------------------------------------------------------

# Welcome to November 2021

An intense **New Moon in Scorpio on the 4<sup>th</sup>**, makes an exact squared connection with the great awakener Uranus, who in turn squares up with the energy of karmic, restructuring Saturn. With passionate, fiery Mars also making a significant contribution, this collaboration looks to bring a dynamic start to the month.

It seems we are called yet again to peel back another layer and recognize those aspects in both our internal and external lives that are still limiting our horizons and potentially blocking us from building a unified future.

**Our Oracle Cards and Runes offer us guidance. The Card of Internal Dialogue** calls us to notice our own inner language and commit to changing anything from within that is sending out a negative request into the universe. **Combined with Perth, the Rune of Initiation**, this combination marks a deeply personal rite of passage on our unique individual pathways to spiritual awakening.

When **the Sun and Mercury unite, exact on the 10<sup>th</sup>**, the following 9 day window brings real opportunity to let go of past grievances and remove any borders that have previously slowed down or inhibited the arrival of solutions that can forge new ways of being in the creation of a more balanced and unified future.

**Our second Oracle Card of Don't Wobble** appearing two months in a row, **alongside Gebo, the Rune of Partnership**, calls us to trust! We are facing tough choices in the midst of a changing world, and yet this card reminds us, that from deep within our higher self knows what we need to do.

When we reach **the Full Moon Eclipse in Taurus on the 19<sup>th</sup>**, Mars, Uranus and Saturn firmly hold this calling for change. The Sun and the Moon collaborate with Jupiter enhancing an energetic of newfound optimism and ideas of expanded possibilities.

**The Sun enters Sagittarius on the 22<sup>nd</sup>** aligning favorably with Mercury, planet of communication and the winged messenger of the gods. This energetic stays with us through to the end of the month offering real space for creative solutions to be found to bring into being, a unified, balanced and fulfilled vision of the future, both personally and collectively.

Associated with the phoenix rising from the ashes, the Rune of Perth speaks of powerful transitions at a deeply personal level. Such changes are necessary for our individual evolution at a level of Soul and mark a profound spiritual period of opportunity to emerge into a space of higher consciousness.

Internal Dialogue
27

We all have an internal dialogue within our mind,
a constant stream of inner conversation.
Is your dialogue kind, supportive and affirming or is it
critical and judgemental, of both yourself and others?
This card asks you to listen to your inner words
and if necessary, take steps to consciously
change your language.

**Additional messages and guidance.**

Words carry power! A charismatic leader can inspire an audience to step up and be the very best version of themselves or inflame an audience into committing acts of atrocity that step over any boundaries of what would constitute a decent human being.

Does your inner dialogue promote love and kindness to both yourself and others, or is it judgmental, critical and harsh?

Almost everyone when they first listen to their internal dialogue will discover a proportion of negativity within this language. Listen to the language in your mind and make a firm commitment to create words of inspiration.

The Rune of Gebo, or Partnership, is also sometimes referred to as A Gift. Its appearance this month calls us to examine our relationship with ourselves and to strengthen our connection with our higher self and the divine. This becomes the source of trust in a fast and changing world

Don't Wobble

13

Are you having a wobble?
Whether a minor one or a Major one this is completely understandable... you are facing tough choices...
but deep inside yourself you know what you need to do!
This card is here to validate your deeper knowing and the decisions that you are making. As you move forwards,
your anxiety will ease and you will refind your balance.

**Additional messages and guidance.**
This card brings a clear message. You are facing tough choices that are raising your levels of anxiety. Whatever your situation, this card is here to validate the decisions and the choices that you are making. You know that something has to change, and deep down you know what you need to do.

It is time to take action.

Find a form of meditation that works for you. Either traditional meditation, or perhaps a walking meditation, where you connect with nature. Whatever you do, take time every day to center yourself, to get still, and to connect with the support of the universe that surrounds you. Let go of any self-doubt and trust your inner knowing.

**1** Monday
Virgo / Libra

**2** Tuesday
Libra

**3** Wednesday
Libra

**4** Thursday
Libra / Scorpio

Super New Moon LA 14.14 – NY 17.14 – London 21.14

**5** Friday
Scorpio

Super New Moon Sydney 08.14 - Auckland 10.14

———————————— Journaling and Notes ————————————

---

**6** Saturday
**Scorpio / Sagittarius**

---

**7** Sunday
**Sagittarius**

**8** Monday
Sagittarius / Capricorn

**9** Tuesday
Capricorn

**10** Wednesday
Capricorn / Aquarius

**11** Thursday
Aquarius

First Quarter Moon

**12** Friday
Aquarius / Pisces

———————————— Journaling and Notes ————————————

--------------------------------------------------------------------------------

**13** Saturday
Pisces

--------------------------------------------------------------------------------

**14** Sunday
Pisces / Aries

---

## 15 Monday
Aries

---

## 16 Tuesday
Aries

---

## 17 Wednesday
Aries / Taurus

---

## 18 Thursday
Taurus

---

## 19 Friday
Taurus / Gemini

---

Full Moon Eclipse LA 00.57 – NY 03.57 – London 08.57 · Sydney 19.57 – Auckland 21.57

---

──────────────── Journaling and Notes ────────────────

----------------------------------------------------------------------

**20** Saturday
Gemini

----------------------------------------------------------------------

**21** Sunday
Gemini

## 22 Monday
Gemini / Cancer

Sun enters Sagittarius

## 23 Tuesday
Cancer

## 24 Wednesday
Cancer / Leo

## 25 Thursday
Leo

USA Thanksgiving Day

## 26 Friday
Leo

———————————— Journaling and Notes ————————————

**27** Saturday
Leo / Virgo

**Last Quarter Moon**

**28** Sunday
Virgo

# Reflections from November

-------------------------------------------------- Journaling & Notes --------------------------------------------------

# Welcome to December 2021

We begin December with **a New moon Eclipse in Sagittarius on the 4th**, with an incredibly powerful mix of energetics that are perfect for manifestation. The connection between motivated Mars, emotional Neptune and transformative Pluto is just flowing, and this energetic continues for the entire month. Eclipse season naturally invites us to meditate and open ourselves to a space of possibility **and Thurisaz, the Rune of Gateway** reinforces this perspective. This Rune asks us to stop and cast our mind back over all we have seen and experienced, and then with gratitude for all we have learned, we can step into the new. **Our Oracle Card of Giving and Receiving**, invites further reflection requesting balance in all our relationships and with **Venus stationing direct moving into retrograde on the 15th**, we are invited to bring our attention to those aspects of our lives that really matter. Set your wishes and open yourself to guidance and hold your vision whilst simultaneously giving it room to grow.

**The Full Moon in Gemini on the 19th** sees Venus align with Pluto inviting deep inner soul searching to illuminate any aspects of our lives that need to come back into balance. **Our second Oracle Card of Allow Yourself to Receive** guides us to release any inner resistances to our own personal entitlement and worthiness. The optimistic influence of Jupiter expands our visions beyond concerns of the ego and invites us to dream of a world that is centered in universal love, and with Mercury and Uranus also communicating well, there is potential for fruitful conversations that help in overcoming resistance to change.

**Ehwaz, the Rune of Movement** acknowledges the overall gathering of energy through this powerful month of manifestation. **The Solstice on the 21st** holds the energy of reflection beautifully and as the earth pauses for breath and **the Sun moves into Capricorn**, use this opportunity to center yourself. It is not uncommon to feel a little discombobulated around these powerful natural shifts in the earth energy around us and with the final exact squaring up of Uranus and Saturn on Christmas Eve, remain grounded and be open to receive guidance for your next steps in your process of personal manifestation.

We end December with Jupiter moving into Pisces, bringing renewed optimism and hope to our dreams and wishes. As we approach a New year and **the first New Moon of 2022 on January 2nd in Capricorn**, take time to reflect and plan for stability and a future that holds a reverence for the unity of all of life.

The Rune of Thurisaz, or Gateway, advises us to contemplate. Reflection and Guidance are needed before proceeding. Pause and review. Lean into a space of gratitude for all that you have experienced both good and bad, this has made you who you are today. You are now ready to proceed

Giving and Receiving.

18

Give and Take is different to Giving and Receiving.
Taking and receiving are not the same.
When we take, whoever we take from may or may not have chosen to give, however, when we receive, choice and respect are an integral part of the exchange.
Let go of any need to Take and embrace the harmony of Giving and Receiving.

**Additional messages and guidance.**
This card asks you to re-evaluate your perspectives of 'Give and Take' within relationships. Are you in a relationship where give and take seems to be out of balance? Are you facing circumstances in which you feel you are giving more than you are receiving and in which your contribution is either undervalued or indeed sometimes not really acknowledged at all?

Take time to reflect on the balance of giving and receiving in all of your relationships and if necessary, make adjustments, including reaching out and discussing this different perspective with all other parties involved.

The Rune of Ehwaz is a Rune of transition and movement and suggests the bettering of any situation. This Rune looks ahead to the future and indicates progress and a gradual moving forwards that will gather momentum and is worthy of our investment.

Allow yourself to Receive

1

One of the greatest blocks in our ability to manifest our
greatest desires is
an inability to allow ourselves to receive.
This card asks that you take some time to identify any
inner beliefs, perceptions and attitudes
that stop you from receiving and one by one,
remove these resistances.

### Additional messages and guidance.

There are many reasons why we block ourselves from receiving, but one thing is certain, it will almost always go back to some event in our past.

It is understandable to be fearful if we have been hurt or damaged by others, but in trying to shut out bad experiences, we also shut out the good ones too, closing ourselves to the possibility of healing. It is time to move beyond your fears. Give yourself permission to receive. If this card is drawn in response to a particular person or situation, this card asks you to lower your defense's and take a risk.

**29** Monday
Virgo / Libra

**30** Tuesday
Libra

**1** Wednesday
Libra / Scorpio

**2** Thursday
Scorpio

**3** Friday
Scorpio / Sagittarius

Super New Moon Eclipse LA 23.43

──────────────── Journaling and Notes ────────────────

**4** Saturday
**Sagittarius**

New moon Eclipse NY 02.43 – London 07.43 – Sydney 18.43 – Auckland 20.43

**5** Sunday
**Sagittarius / Capricorn**

**6** Monday
Capricorn

**7** Tuesday
Capricorn / Aquarius

**8** Wednesday
Aquarius

**9** Thursday
Aquarius / Pisces

**10** Friday
Pisces

—————————— Journaling and Notes ——————————

- - - - - - - - - - - - - - - - - - - - - - - - - - - - - - - - - - - - - - - - - - - - - - - - - - - -

## 11 Saturday
**Pisces / Aries**

**First Quarter Moon**

- - - - - - - - - - - - - - - - - - - - - - - - - - - - - - - - - - - - - - - - - - - - - - - - - - - -

## 12 Sunday
**Aries**

**13** Monday
Aries

**14** Tuesday
Aries / Taurus

**15** Wednesday
Taurus

**16** Thursday
Taurus / Gemini

**17** Friday
Gemini

———————— Journaling and Notes ————————

-------------------------------------------------------------------------------

## 18 Saturday
**Gemini**

**Full Moon LA 20.35 – NY 23.35**
-------------------------------------------------------------------------------

## 19 Sunday
**Gemini / Cancer**

**Venus Retrograde until 29th January 2022**
**Full Moon London 04.35 - Sydney 15.35 – Auckland 17.35**
-------------------------------------------------------------------------------

**20** Monday
Cancer

**21** Tuesday
Cancer / Leo

Winter Solstice Northern Hemisphere – Summer Solstice Southern Hemisphere

**22** Wednesday
Leo

Sun enters Capricorn

**23** Thursday
Leo

**24** Friday
Leo / Virgo

Daily Collective Prayer Begins – 1 Minute of Silent Prayer 7pm daily until 29th December
Christmas eve

——————————— Journaling and Notes ———————————

---

**25** Saturday
Virgo

Christmas Day

---

**26** Sunday
Virgo / Leo

Boxing Day

---

## 27 Monday
Libra

UK Christmas Day Substitute Bank Holiday
Last Quarter Moon

## 28 Tuesday
Libra / Scorpio

UK Boxing Day Substitute Bank Holiday

## 29 Wednesday
Scorpio

Daily Collective Prayer Ends Today – Thank you

## 30 Thursday
Scorpio / Sagittarius

## 31 Friday
Sagittarius

January 2022
======

—————————— Journaling and Notes ——————————

-----------------------------------------------------------------------

**1** Saturday
**Sagittarius / Capricorn**

-----------------------------------------------------------------------

**2** Sunday
**Capricorn**

New Moon LA 10.33 – NY 13.33 – London 18.33
Monday 3rd January - Sydney 05.33 – Auckland 07.33
-----------------------------------------------------------------------

-------------------------------------------------- Journaling & Notes --------------------------------------------------

-------------------------------------------------- Journaling & Notes --------------------------------------------------

**Blessings to you for the coming year of 2022**

**The Art of Manifestation Oracle Cards**

The Art of Manifestation Oracle Cards featured in this diary are available to buy from the A-Z store at; https://www.azemotionalhealth.store/

They are also available on Amazon.

## About the Author

Jenny Florence is a best-selling Author and her professional career as an Accredited BACP, UKRC Registered Counsellor spanned over 28 years working with individuals, couples and teams.

Her books include;

7 Steps to Spiritual Empathy – Learn to Listen, Change your Life! Mindfulness meets Emotional Awareness - 7 Steps to Learn the Language of your Emotions and the I Choose Love Series which includes I Choose Love – the A-Z Guidebook for the Spiritual Warrior, the Art of Manifestation Astro-Moon Diary and Journal and the Art of Manifestation Oracle Cards.

Her books are available from Amazon or from the A-Z of Emotional Health online Store.

https://www.azemotionalhealth.store/

She first began reading Tarot cards as a teenager and has also studied astrology. She posts free weekly and bi-monthly readings on her YouTube Channel which align with the natural cycles of the Moon.

She is the founder and creator of the A-Z of Emotional Health on-line Video Library, a free Public Resource, dedicated to understanding Emotional and Mental Wellness from a holistic perspective.

For more information visit her Free on-line Library;
https://www.azemotionalhealth.com/


Or follow her on Social Media;

YouTube - http://www.youtube.com/c/AZEmotionalHealth

Facebook - https://www.facebook.com/azofemotionalhealth/

Printed in Great Britain
by Amazon